Edward Francis Wilson

Missionary Work among the Ojebway Indians

Edward Francis Wilson

Missionary Work among the Ojebway Indians

ISBN/EAN: 9783337060060

Printed in Europe, USA, Canada, Australia, Japan

Cover: Foto ©ninafisch / pixelio.de

More available books at **www.hansebooks.com**

MISSIONARY WORK

AMONG

THE OJEBWAY INDIANS.

BY THE

REV. EDWARD F. WILSON.

PUBLISHED UNDER THE DIRECTION OF THE TRACT COMMITTEE.

LONDON:
SOCIETY FOR PROMOTING CHRISTIAN KNOWLEDGE,
NORTHUMBERLAND AVENUE, CHARING CROSS, W.C.;
43, QUEEN VICTORIA STREET, E.C.;
26, ST. GEORGE'S PLACE, HYDE PARK CORNER, S.W.
BRIGHTON: 135, NORTH STREET.
NEW YORK: E. & J. B. YOUNG & CO.
1886.

CONTENTS.

CHAP.		PAGE
	INTRODUCTION.	
I.	HOW IT CAME ABOUT THAT I WENT TO CANADA	13
II.	FIRST MISSIONARY EXPERIENCES	16
III.	OUR ARRIVAL AT SARNIA	21
IV.	KETTLE POINT	26
V.	INDIAN NAMES GIVEN	31
VI.	CHRISTMAS ON THE RESERVE	35
VII.	MISSION WORK AT SARNIA	39
VIII.	THE BISHOP'S VISIT	45
IX.	FIRST VISIT TO GARDEN RIVER	49
X.	BAPTISM OF PAGAN INDIANS	55
XI.	THE RED RIVER EXPEDITION	60
XII.	CHANGES IN PROSPECT	69
XIII.	ROUGHING IT	73
XIV.	CHIEF LITTLE PINE	79
XV.	OUR FIRST WINTER IN ALGOMA	85
XVI.	CHIEF BUHKWUJJENENE'S MISSION	92
XVII.	AN INDIAN CHIEF IN ENGLAND	101
XVIII.	A TRIAL OF FAITH	108
XIX.	LEARNING TO KNOW MY PEOPLE	113
XX.	A WEDDING AND A DEATH	121
XXI.	THE OPENING OF THE FIRST SHINGWAUK HOME	125
XXII.	FIRE! FIRE!	130
XXIII.	AFTER THE FIRE	135
XXIV.	PROSPECTS OF RE-BUILDING	140
XXV.	LAYING THE FOUNDATION STONE	145
XXVI.	A TRIP TO BATCHEEWAUNING	149
XXVII.	THE WINTER OF 1874-5	154

CONTENTS.

CHAP.		PAGE
XXVIII.	THE NEW SHINGWAUK HOME	161
XXIX.	RUNAWAY BOYS	166
XXX.	CHARLIE AND BEN	171
XXXI.	A TRIP UP LAKE SUPERIOR	177
XXXII.	COASTING AND CAMPING	185
XXXIII.	UP THE NEEPIGON RIVER	188
XXXIV.	THIRTY YEARS WAITING FOR A MISSIONARY	198
XXXV.	THE PAGAN BOY—NINGWINNENA	205
XXXVI.	BAPTIZED—BURIED	212
XXXVII.	THE WAWANOSH HOME	219
XXXVIII.	A SAD WINTER	224
XXXIX.	WILLIAM SAHGUCHEWAY	229
XL.	OUR INDIAN HOMES	239
XLI.	A POW-WOW AT GARDEN RIVER	246
XLII.	GLAD TIDINGS FROM NEEPIGON	250

PREFACE.

 A FEW words addressed by the Bishop of Algoma to the Provincial Synod may form a suitable preface to this little book, which aspires to no literary pretensions, but is just a simple and unvarnished narrative of Missionary experience among the Red Indians of Lake Superior, in the Algoma Diocese.

"The invaluable Institutions at Sault Ste. Marie still continue their blessed work of educating and Christianizing the rising generation of Ojebways. Founded in a spirit of faith, hope, and charity,—carrying out a sound system of education, and in the past 'approved of God' by many signs and tokens, the friends of these two 'Homes' may still rally round them with unshaken confidence. Their history, like that of the Christian Church itself, has been marked by not a few fluctuations, but their record has been one of permanent and undoubted usefulness.

"Only a person deeply interested and directly engaged in the work, as the Rev. E. F. Wilson is, can understand the force of the difficulties to be encountered from the ineradicable scepticism of Indian parents as to the disinterestedness of our intentions with regard to their children; the tendency of the children to rebel against the necessary restraints imposed on their liberty; the reluctance of parents to leave their children in the 'Home' for a period sufficiently long for the formation of permanent habits of industry, and fixed principles of right; the constitutional unhealthiness of Indian children, terminating, as it has here in a few cases, in death; the all but impossibility of obtaining helpers for subordinate positions, such as teacher or servant, who regard the question of the evangelization of the Indian from any higher stand-point than the financial.

"Against this formidable array of obstacles Mr. Wilson has not only struggled, but struggled successfully, till now these two Institutions, over which he has watched with all the jealous vigilance of a mother watching her first-born child, stand on a basis of acknowledged success, as two centres for the diffusion of Gospel light and blessing among the children of a people who have been long 'sitting in darkness, and the shadow of death.' During the past year sundry improvements have been made in the Shingwauk Home, which will largely increase the comfort of the occupants. The most notable event, however, to be recorded in this connection is the completion and consecration of the 'Bishop Fauquier Memorial Chapel,' a beautiful and truly ecclesiastical structure, designed, in even its minutest details, by Mr. Wilson, and erected by means of

PREFACE.

A FEW words addressed by the Bishop of Algoma to the Provincial Synod may form a suitable preface to this little book, which aspires to no literary pretensions, but is just a simple and unvarnished narrative of Missionary experience among the Red Indians of Lake Superior, in the Algoma Diocese.

"The invaluable Institutions at Sault Ste. Marie still continue their blessed work of educating and Christianizing the rising generation of Ojebways. Founded in a spirit of faith, hope, and charity,—carrying out a sound system of education, and in the past 'approved of God' by many signs and tokens, the friends of these two 'Homes' may still rally round them with unshaken confidence. Their history, like that of the Christian Church itself, has been marked by not a few fluctuations, but their record has been one of permanent and undoubted usefulness.

"Only a person deeply interested and directly engaged in the work, as the Rev. E. F. Wilson is, can understand the force of the difficulties to be encountered from the ineradicable scepticism of Indian parents as to the disinterestedness of our intentions with regard to their children; the tendency of the children to rebel against the necessary restraints imposed on their liberty; the reluctance of parents to leave their children in the 'Home' for a period sufficiently long for the formation of permanent habits of industry, and fixed principles of right; the constitutional unhealthiness of Indian children, terminating, as it has here in a few cases, in death; the all but impossibility of obtaining helpers for subordinate positions, such as teacher or servant, who regard the question of the evangelization of the Indian from any higher stand-point than the financial.

"Against this formidable array of obstacles Mr. Wilson has not only struggled, but struggled successfully, till now these two Institutions, over which he has watched with all the jealous vigilance of a mother watching her first-born child, stand on a basis of acknowledged success, as two centres for the diffusion of Gospel light and blessing among the children of a people who have been long 'sitting in darkness, and the shadow of death.' During the past year sundry improvements have been made in the Shingwauk Home, which will largely increase the comfort of the occupants. The most notable event, however, to be recorded in this connection is the completion and consecration of the 'Bishop Fauquier Memorial Chapel,' a beautiful and truly ecclesiastical structure, designed, in even its minutest details, by Mr. Wilson, and erected by means of funds sent mainly from England, in response to his earnest appeals for some enduring and useful memorial of the life and labours of the late revered Bishop of this diocese. Long may it stand, as a hallowed centre for the diffusion of Gospel light among hundreds yet unborn, of the Indian tribes he loved so well."

MISSIONARY WORK AMONG THE OJEBWAY INDIANS.

INTRODUCTORY.

THE largest freshwater lake in the world is Lake Superior, through the centre of which runs the boundary line between the United States of America and the Dominion of Canada. The Indians call it the "Ojebway Kecheguramee," that is—literally translated—the Great water of the Ojebways, or as they are often called the Chippeways.

The Ojebways are an extensive Indian tribe spreading over a large part of Canada, the Northern States, and the North West; specimens of their language and customs appear in Longfellow's song of Hiawatha. Lake Superior may be regarded as the centre of their ancient possessions. Along its northern shores, and back into the interior they still roam in wild freedom, hunting, and fishing, and paddling their birch-bark canoes;—but in more civilized places, they are confined to reserved lands set apart for them by the Dominion Government, and many of them now gain their living by farming or by working for the neighbouring white people.

The Ojebway Indians are now just in that transition stage in which they particularly require a helping hand to lift them up to a respectable position in life, and to afford them the means of gaining their livelihood as a civilised Christian people. As one of their own Chiefs has said, "the time is passed for my people to live by hunting and fishing as our forefathers used to do; if we are to continue to exist at all we must learn to gain our living in the same way as the white people."

It is with the view of making the wants of these poor people known, and of increasing the interest in a work which amid many difficulties, has for the past ten years been carried on among them, that these pages are written. The writer will tell what have been his experiences with the Indians since he first came to settle among them as a Missionary, and will describe how God in His providence gradually opened the way for him, how dangers were met, and difficulties overcome, and how in the end two Institutions for the Christian training and civilization of Indian children were brought into existence; the one called the *Shingwauk Home*, with accommodation for about seventy Indian boys, and the other called the *Waranosh Home*, with room for about thirty Indian girls, —both of them built, and now in active operation, at Sault Ste. Marie, Ontario, at the south-eastern extremity of Lake Superior.

CHAPTER I.

How it came about that I went to Canada.

ALL things are wonderfully ordered for us by God. Such has been my experience for a long time past. If only we will wait and watch, the way will open for us.

Where shall I begin with my history as a Missionary? When I was a child, it was my mother's hope and wish that I should bear the glad tidings of the Gospel to distant lands. She was a Missionary in heart herself, and it was her earnest desire that one of her boys would grow up to devote himself to that most blessed work.

However there seemed little likelihood of her wishes being fulfilled. I disliked the idea of going to Oxford as my brothers had done. A wild free life away from the restraints of civilization was my idea of happiness, and after studying agriculture for a year or two in England, I bade farewell to my native shores and started for Canada.

Then God took me in hand. I had been only three days in the country when He put it into my heart to become a Missionary. The impulse came suddenly, irresistibly. In a few days it was all settled. Farming was given up, and I entered upon my course as a theological student. That same summer I spent a month or six weeks on an Indian Reserve, and became, as people would say, infatuated with the Indians. For this and other reasons, I preferred remaining in Canada that I might study for the ministry, to returning to England; and whenever opportunity allowed, I paid a visit to some Indian Reserve, or went on an exploring tour up the great lakes.

After rather more than two years' preparation, I returned to England, and in December, 1867, was ordained deacon at the Chapel Royal, by the Bishop of London, Dr. Tait, afterwards Archbishop of Canterbury.

Shortly after this, it was arranged that I should go out again to Canada as a Missionary to the Ojebway Indians, under the auspices of the Church Missionary Society, the Rev. Henry Venn being then Hon. Secretary, and on July 1, 1868, accompanied by my wife and an old faithful servant named Jane, we started for Canada.

My wife, accustomed to the refinement and comforts of a beautiful old rectory home in Gloucestershire, knew not whither she was going. — she had never been out of England before, and all was new and strange to her. Indeed, I for my part was going out also, "not knowing whither I went." Whether our lot would be cast in one of the older and more civilised dioceses of Canada, or whether we should find a home on the very outskirts of civilization, I knew not. My instructions from the Church Missionary Society Committee, were simply to go first to London, Ont., where the late Bishop of Huron (Dr. Cronyn) then lived, and from thence to travel around and select what might seem to be the best spot to make the centre for a new mission. We had thought of Cape Croker on the Georgian Bay, and we had thought of Michipicoten, on Lake Superior, — but nothing could be settled until after our arrival in Canada, and as for my wife she was content to go with me wherever I went.

We had a splendid view of icebergs on the eighth day of our voyage. It was a clear, keen morning reminding one of Christmas time, the sailors were washing the decks and all looked merry and bright, and around on all sides were icebergs of every size and shape, some looking like great sea monsters bobbing up and down on the water, others as if a large extent of Dover Cliff were floating past. Twenty-seven we counted at one time, and during the morning fully 150 must have passed us. "Ah,' said an old sailor, "if one of them had touched us, this ship wouldn't be here." Then came the excitement of whales, spouting in the deep, and at 10 a.m., on July 10th, the rocky coast of Belle Isle was in sight.

When we landed at Quebec, the heat was intense, the glass standing at 99° in the shade. My wife's first experiences of Canada are described in a letter home, dated from London, Ont., July 22nd, '68. "At 4 p.m. we left Quebec and started by boat for Montreal. The boats for the lakes and river are simply splendid,—such large handsome saloons and everything very nice, except that we had only one small towel between us and very little water. After leaving Montreal we had to go through a succession of locks which was slow work and made us feel the heat very much. On Wednesday it was a little cooler, and we were able to enjoy the most lovely scenery I had ever beheld, 'the thousand isles,'—that alone is quite worth coming out for. From Hamilton we took train to London. No one can remember such a summer before, for the last three weeks the glass has been standing at between 103° and 99° except in the evening, when we think it cold if it goes down to 80°. The boarding-house we are in is cool and clean and quite English-like about a mile from the so-called town."

Almost immediately after settling in at our

London boarding-house I started on my first Missionary tour, the object being to choose a spot suitable for the centre of our Mission.

CHAPTER II.

First Missionary Experiences.

My first service among the Indians was held in a little log-house on the Indian Reserve, at Sarnia (south of Lake Huron), on Sunday, July 26th. Twenty-two Indians of the Ojebway tribe were present. They all seemed most anxious to have a Church of England Mission established in their midst, as many of them, inclusive of their venerable old chief, Wawanosh, were already members of the Church, and had been from time to time visited by a Missionary. I promised to visit them again on my return from other Indian settlements and see what could be done.

The following day, Monday, I took train to Toronto, and thence to Collingwood, from which place I intended to branch off to Owen Sound and visit the Cape Croker and Saugeen Indians. I had with me as interpreter a young Indian named Andrew Jacobs, his Indian name being Wagimah-wishkung, and for short I called him Wagimah. At Owen Sound we met with some Cape Croker Indians, and engaged their boat and two men to take us the following day to their settlement, about forty miles up the Lake Shore.

Soon after four the next morning we were up and dressed, and an hour later were on our way. It was fine, but rather foggy, and the sun scarcely visible through the mist. Not a breath of wind was stirring, so we had to keep to our oars, sometimes one and sometimes another rowing. At noon we reached Commodore Point, and put in for about an hour, spending our time in eating raspberries, which were growing in the greatest profusion, and bathing in the bay. Then on we pushed again, past Griffith's Island, White Cloud Island, and King's Point, and arrived at length, after a voyage of eight hours, at Cape Croker. We found that there were about 350 Ojebway Indians in the place, the majority of whom were Roman Catholics or Methodists; they had good houses, some log, but mostly neat little frame weather-boarded buildings; the land, however, was much neglected, very little attempt being made at farming. A Church of England service was conducted on Sundays by an Indian Catechist named Angus. The Chief's name was Tabegwun. On the day after our arrival I held a meeting with the Indians, and explained to them my object in coming to visit them, and began by reading the Scriptures, and preaching to them, and baptizing one or two children. They gave me the names of twenty-six persons who professed to belong to the Church of England, and were desirous of having a Mission established among them. During our stay we were guests at Mr. Angus's house, a clean, respectable dwelling, and were regaled with venison and huckleberry pie.

The next Indian Reserve that we visited was Saugeen. To reach this place we had to return by boat to Owen Sound, and then go across country in a westerly direction to the shores of Lake Huron. The journey was accomplished by "buggy." We started at 4 a.m. on the morning of July 31st, and stopped to have our breakfast on the roadside about 7 o'clock, sitting one at each end of a log facing each other, our plates and cups in front of us. We reached the Indian village at 8.30 a.m., and went to the house of the chief whose name was Madwayosh. Only his wife was at home, but we learnt all that we wanted from her. There were about 250 Ojebway Indians on this Reserve, and nearly all Methodists. They had a resident Methodist Missionary and a place of worship in course of erection. I at once came to the conclusion that it would be unsuitable for us to attempt any Mission work in this place; and when we bade adieu to Mrs. Madwayosh. we drove on to the Sauble Reserve, five miles further. A most dreadful road it was the whole way. We had both to get down and lead the horse more than half the distance, and then our traps were in the most imminent danger of jumping out as the buggy went jolting and rolling on over huge boulders and logs and stumps. It took us over two hours to reach the place, and when we got there, rain was coming down in torrents. We inquired for Waubesee's house, he being a member of the Church, and after some trouble we at length found it, but it lay back at a distance from the road, with only a trail leading to it, so we had to take the horse out of the buggy and lead him after us. The little house, made entirely of bark, stood in the most picturesque spot, surrounded by lofty pines. Near the house was a calf shed, into which we tried to squeeze our horse, but he would not go, so we had to take him to a stable about a mile off.

Waubesee and his family received us very warmly. They said there used to be a great many Church people among them, but no missionary had been to see them for many years, and now all who had belonged to the Church were either gone away into the States, or had joined the Methodists. Waubesee, his wife, children, and grandchildren, numbered eighteen in all, and he said that the whole number of Indians on the Reserve was about 250. He seemed to be an intelligent man, and got out his Ojebway prayer-book and Testament to show us. Before we left, the family and a few others were called together, and we had reading and prayer, and I gave them a short address, Wagimah acting as my interpreter.

We now had to drive to Southampton, a distance of eight miles, and it was 6.30 p.m. when we reached it. My interpreter left me here to return to his home by the way we had come, and I took steamboat to Goderich, and from thence by train to London, where I rejoined my wife.

My next trip was to Brantford, and my wife accompanied me. We started on the 5th of August, and on our arrival there, were hospitably entertained at the Rev. Mr. Nelles' house. From there I went to visit the Indians on the New Credit Reserve, a considerable distance off. I called on Chief Sawyer, a tall, fine man, with a sensible-looking face. He said there were about 300 Ojebway Indians on the Reserve, and that many of them were most desirous of having a Church of England teacher.

The result of all these visits was, that after much earnest prayer for Divine guidance, we finally decided upon making Sarnia our headquarters, and on the 8th of August I paid a second visit to the Indians there, and told them that I had decided to come and live amongst them. We expected there would be a little difficulty at first, as the Methodists were already in the field, and might oppose our coming; but as the Chief and quite a large number of the people were already professed members of the Church, having been frequently visited by the Rev. Mr. Chase, the native minister at Muncy Town, it seemed only fair that their oft-repeated petition to the Bishop of Huron should be attended to, and that a Church of England Mission should be established among them. On the 11th of August a Council was held, at which some fifty Indians attended. They sat about indiscriminately on benches, some smoking their pipes, others chewing tobacco. In a few plain words I told them how it was my own earnest desire to devote myself as a Missionary to the Indians, and how I had been sent by a great Society in England to search out and teach the Ojebway Indians of the western part of Canada. I had already, I said, visited the Indians of Cape Croker, Saugeen, Sauble, and the Grand River, and had now made up my mind to make Sarnia my head-quarters, and to build a church in their midst. We would not, I said, put up a large expensive one,—we would begin with a small rough one, and see how we got on,—an Indian had already promised us land, and now I wanted all Indians whose hearts were in the work to lend us a helping hand and aid in erecting the church; it should be a small log building, and cost not more than 200 dollars. Mr. Chase was also present, and spoke very nicely after I had finished. After the council was over I proposed to Mr. Chase and a few other Indians that we should kneel down and ask God's blessing, and so we knelt down and laid our case before God and asked Him to guide and direct us, and to incline the hearts of the Indians to favour our undertaking. Next morning I returned to London, and on the 15th we moved down to Sarnia, and took up our abode temporarily at Mrs. Walker's boarding-house.

CHAPTER III.

Our Arrival at Sarnia.

Mrs. Walker's boarding-house was a frame, white-painted house situate in the town of Sarnia, a little way back from the main street. The Indian Reserve almost adjoined the town, so that a quarter of an hour's walk would take us on to their land. In front of the town and flowing down past the Indian Reserve is the broad river St. Clair, connecting Lake Huron with Lake Erie, its banks on the Canadian side dotted over with the boats and fishing nets of the Indians.

I at once invested in a horse and buggy, and also engaged Wagimah as my interpreter. I could already read the service in Indian, but required an interpreter's aid for conversing with the people and preaching. Our Sunday services were held in a vacant log hut, in which we had a little desk rigged up and some forms arranged as seats. On my first Sunday among them I baptized two children, an infant in arms named Jacob Gray, and a child of four or five named Thomas Winter. Both of these boys some nine or ten years afterwards became pupils at the Shingwauk Home.

Our great object now was to build a log church and also a Mission house for our own use with as little delay as possible. There was a quaint old Indian, or rather half-breed, for he was partly French, with whom I had some conversation in regard to our proposed operations. "Well, Mr. Leviere," I said to him one day, "what do you think the Indians will be willing to do? Will they cut down the trees,—square and haul the logs?" "I have been thinking about it a good deal," he replied. "You want a church forty feet long; this will take a great many logs, not much black ash now in the bush. I don't think, Sir, you will find enough trees. Why not build a frame church? If you build frame, Indians get out logs, fit the frame one day, raise building next day, board it next day, get done quick; not cost much money, cost perhaps $100, not much money." "Now, supposing we were to do this, what would the Indians be willing to give? Would they work without pay? I want the white people to see that the Indians are really in earnest; I should like to point to our church and say, 'The Indians built this church without pay, because it was their wish to build a house to God.' Do you think the Indians are ready to do this? Are you ready to give a helping hand yourself?" "Oh, indeed, Sir, yes! I mean to work, and keep on working till it is finished; I think there are many who will do so too, perhaps ten or fifteen altogether; we shall want no pay, only provisions."

Our chief source of discouragement at this time

was the opposition of the Methodist party, who were considerably in the majority on the Reserve. As Indian land is held in common by all the members of the band, we were at one time in fear that we might be prevented from building. A petition was sent to Government, and correspondence entered into with the Indian Department, and in the end we were permitted to take possession of one acre of land on the lot of a Church Indian named Antoine Rodd. The opposition, however, was very bitter and rather depressing, and our opponents went so far as to threaten to deprive the old Chief, Wawanosh, of his chieftainship.

On the other hand, we had every encouragement from the conduct of our own Indians. The opposition that they met with only seemed to make them more determined to stand by us and assist in the establishment of the Mission. Directly the land question was settled, three or four of them started back in the bush with their axes, to fell the trees and hew and square the timbers for the frame-work of the church, and I heard that the old Chief had been to the Indian Agent's office and borrowed ten dollars of the Annuity-money to pay a professed hewer, as none of themselves were good hands at such work. This, I told them, was more than I expected of them; if they would give their labour, that was all that I asked; but no, they would not be dissuaded; they were quite determined, they said, to raise the frame-work unaided, and they would much rather themselves pay for any labour they might have to employ.

The "Raising" took place on the 22nd of September. About fifty Indians were present, and all took part more or less in the work. In the afternoon two teams arrived from the town with a large party of ladies and gentlemen, well supplied with baskets of provisions for a feast, which they had kindly arranged to give the Indians at the conclusion of their work. The roughly extemporised tables looked most inviting when all was spread out, and two or three of the Indian women were most active and clever in getting everything ready. When the feast was over the Indians gathered in a circle, and I expressed to them my pleasure that we had got thus far with our work, and told them that I hoped we should soon now, with God's blessing, have our little church open and ready for service. Joseph Wawanosh on behalf of his father, the old Chief, then expressed his gratitude that a Missionary had at length come among them, and that a church was in course of erection. After this we concluded with a short service in the Ojebway language.

It was very encouraging to me to find that our cause was being taken up in England; a little circular had been printed and distributed, and by the middle of October £64 had been contributed towards the erection of our Mission buildings.

In the meantime I was holding service regularly every Sunday in the vacant log cottage with an average attendance of from twenty to thirty Indians, and during the week I visited a good deal among the people, my interpreter usually accompanying me. I had prepared a little pocket companion containing passages of Scripture, copied from the Ojebway Testament, sentences of familiar conversation, and Indian prayers and collects. With the help of this little book I was able to make myself understood by the Indians, and soon became almost independent of an interpreter. I had a plan of the Indian Reserve, and usually steered my way through the bush with my compass, taking little notice of the rough corduroy tracks and Indian trails which never seemed to lead to the right place.

One of these expeditions I will briefly describe:

I wanted to find old Widow Kwakegwah's house, which lay about two miles back through the bush in a south-easterly direction. Wagimah was with me and, leaving the river road, we plunged back at once into the bush without either path or track, and steered our way by my compass. Sometimes it lay through a thick growth of young saplings, which bent aside as we pushed our way through; sometimes over a mass of decaying logs and upheaved roots; sometimes through long grass and swamp up to our knees; occasionally we came to a fallen tree, which we had to clamber over or under. Once or twice we came upon a little log hut standing in the midst of a small clearing, sometimes empty with door bolted, at other times showing signs of occupation. Into one of these we entered; it was a tiny log shanty, with a patch of Indian corn and potatoes enclosed by a snake fence. We pushed open the door, a fire was burning on the hearth, and in a corner was a blanket enveloping something that might be human. I told Wagimah to touch it, he did so, and the bundle moved, part of the blanket wriggled back and a woman's face appeared. She said she was sick, and that no one had been to visit her. We staid and had a little conversation, and then as it was getting late, hurried on to Widow Kwakegwah's. The old woman, who had a very pleasant, honest-looking face, gave us quite a hearty reception. I got her to tell me the number of her children and grand-children, and then taking up her Ojebway Testament read a few verses from St. John iii, and spoke a few words which Wagimah interpreted, after which we knelt for prayer. After this we visited Peter Gray, with his wife and family of eight children; they lived in a small log hut, and there was no glass in the windows. It was now five p.m. and we started on our two miles' trudge back to Antoine Rodds' house, where I had left my buggy, and then drove back to the town.

CHAPTER IV.

KETTLE POINT.

BESIDES the four hundred Indians on the Sarnia Reserve, there were about one hundred more living at Kettle Point, thirty miles distant, on the eastern shore of Lake Huron. I had not been long settled at Sarnia, when, in company with my interpreter, I started on a first visit to these people. I will describe the journey.

Taking the railway as far as Forest, we had to walk on a distance of eight or nine miles. Neither of us knew the country, but a couple of Indians, whom we happened to fall in with, showed us the way.

It was nearly two o'clock when we reached David Sahpah's house. We found the Indians most hospitable; some of them were Methodists, some still pagans, and others members of the Church. They were most desirous of having a Church Mission established among them, as there was no school for their children and no regular services held. Not a single individual, man, woman, or child, could read or write. They were very anxious to have a school-house built and a schoolmaster sent to teach them, indeed some of them had already got out logs with the view of building a school. The Chief's name was Ahbettuhwahnuhgund (Half a Cloud), a fine, broad-shouldered, intelligent-looking man, but still a pagan, although he had had several of his children baptized in the Church. There was also a large family named Shaukeens, all of whom were pagans, and several others. They seemed, however, to have advanced more in their farming operations than the Sarnia Indians. The Chief had a capital house with several rooms in it, an orchard full of apples and cherries, and well-cultivated fields. In the evening we had service at David Sahpah's house, and then I spoke to the Indians and proposed that we should at once commence a fortnightly school among them, myself and my interpreter taking it alternately. There was an empty log-house which they said we could use, and they all seemed pleased at the proposal, and said that they would send their children to be taught.

We had to start at 3.30 a.m. next morning to catch the early train for Sarnia. It was a clear starlight night when we emerged from the hospitable shelter of an Indian's log-house and started on our pilgrimage through the bush. There was no moon, and we had some difficulty in groping our way. Wagimah went first, and slowly and cautiously we proceeded, carrying our wraps and satchels with us. However, with all our care, we had soon lost our way, and found ourselves stumbling along over a potato patch, without having the least idea where we were. For nearly an hour we were wandering about, when at length we came once more upon a beaten track; but whether it was the right one or not we could not tell. However we followed it, and almost before we were aware we found ourselves out of the bush and standing on a broad clay road, and at length we arrived at Forest Station in good time for the cars to Sarnia.

After this we visited Kettle Point every fortnight, and many were the amusing incidents connected with those trips. Sometimes I drove the whole distance in my own trap, at other times took train to Forest or Widder, and some of the Indians would meet me with a waggon or sleigh, as the case might be, at the Station. It was on the 9th of September that we commenced our school in the vacant log-house. We began with A, B, C, as no one yet knew anything. There were eleven children and five adults present. I was amused in the evening to see a game of draughts going on, on a log outside the Chief's house; the draught-board was a flat part of the log with squares carved out on its surface, the black men were squares of pumpkin rind with green side up, the white men the same with the green side down. That night we slept at Adam Sahpah's house.

Our sleeping places on these Kettle Point expeditions were various. One bitterly cold night in the late autumn, I remember, passing in a little boarded shanty used as a workshop. We were nearly perished in the morning, and were glad to get inside David Sahpah's comfortable log-house; a huge fire was blazing on the hearth, and the Indian women all busy, some with their pots and frying-pans, boiling potatoes and baking cakes, others dressing and cleaning the children. Mrs. Ahbettuhwahnuhgund gave me a chair, and down

I sat by the blazing fire and gazed with a feeling of happy contentment into the yellow flames. The scene was certainly a novel one. In a dark corner by the chimney sat a dirty old couple on the couch where they had been passing the night; they were visitors from Muncey Town, and were staying a few nights only at Kettle Point. The old woman lighted up her pipe, and whiffed away with her eyes half shut; after enjoying it for about twenty minutes or so, her old husband thought she had had enough, and taking it from her put it in his own mouth and had his whiff. When he had done, he restored it again to his wife. Underneath another old bedstead were a couple of large dogs, which occasionally let their voices be heard in a dispute; some of the stones on one side of the fire-place had broken away, making a little window through which the dogs could reach the fire, and it was amusing to see how they put their noses and paws through the opening and warmed themselves just like human beings. Down in another corner sat an antiquated old woman enveloped in a blanket, and in vain endeavouring to comfort a little fat boy of about ten months who was crying, as only children know how to cry, for his mother. Finding that she could not content the baby, she at length got up, and taking off her blanket, put one end of it round the baby's shoulders, tucked the ends under its arms, and then with one sweep placed baby and blanket together on her back, and with one or two pulls once more got the blanket wrapped completely round her, and the little fat boy snugly ensconced between her shoulders; then she marched off to give him an airing. The bigger children were set to clean themselves, a tin bowl of water and a towel being given them in turns. I was wondering whether my turn would come, when Mrs. Ahbettuhwahnuhgund, having once more filled the bowl, addressed me with the words, " Maund'uhpe," which in polite English would mean, " Here you are!" " Ah, meegwach, ahpecte "—" thank you kindly "—said I, and forthwith began my ablutions, while the children stood around me in wonderment.

One night I slept with a pig. It was a vacant room in the Chief's new house. After our services were over and we had had supper, Mrs. Ahbettuhwahnuhgund took a clean blanket on her shoulder and a lantern in her hand, and calling me to follow led me to the apartment. There was a bedstead with a mattress on it in a corner, and on two chairs in the middle of the room lay a pig which had been killed the day before. Early next morning, before I was fully awake, the door opened, and Mrs. Ahbettuhwahnuhgund appeared with a knife in her hand. What could she want at this hour in the morning? I opened one eye to see. Her back was turned to me, and I could not distinguish what she was doing, but I heard a slicing and cutting and wheezing. Then the good lady turned round, and closing the eye I had opened I did not venture to look out again till the door was shut, and Mrs. Ahbettuhwahnuhgund departed; then I peeped out from my rug—poor piggy was minus one leg! Next time I saw the missing limb it was steaming on the breakfast table!

I must not make this chapter longer. By-and-bye I shall tell of the baptism of the Chief and several other of the pagan Indians of this place. Suffice it to say now that our little school kept nicely together, and services were held either by myself or my interpreter every fortnight. In a little more than a year's time we had the satisfaction of seeing both a school-church and a master's residence erected, and a catechist placed in charge of the station.

CHAPTER V.

Indian Names Given.

It is a custom with the Indians to bestow Indian names upon missionaries and others who come to work among them, in order to make them, as it were, one with themselves. We had not been many months resident in Sarnia before we received an invitation from the pagan Chief at Kettle Point, to come to a grand feast which the Indians were preparing in our honour at that place, and to receive Indian names by which we should be incorporated into the Ojebway tribe.

It was one of the coldest of winter days when we started, the glass very low, a high wind, and the snow whirling through the air in blinding clouds. We went by train to Forest, and there Ahbettuhwahnuhgund met us with his sleigh. It was just a common box sleigh with two seats, and the bottom filled with straw, and two horses to pull us. We were all bundled up in rugs and blankets and wraps; the Chief, who was driving, had his head completely smothered up in a bright blue shawl belonging to his wife, and wrapped so many times round that he was as wide at the top of his eyes as at his shoulders. The only one of the party who appeared careless about the cold was an Indian named Garchees, who had come with us from Sarnia, and he sat with his feet hanging over the side of the sleigh; however, when we asked him how it was that he did not feel the cold, he replied with a grin, " Moccasins no cold,—white man boot cold,—ice!—two pair socks under moccasins me—big blanket too!" In about an hour and a half we arrived at the Chief's house; it was the first time my wife had been to Kettle Point, and she was very much pleased to make acquaintance with the Indians of whom she had often heard, and who had sent her presents of apples and cherries from their orchards. She had brought with her a few small gifts for the children, with which they were much delighted. A little boy named Isaac had a sugar-dog given to him; he soon had its nose in close quarters with his mouth, and the people laughed to see it disappearing. Indians are nearly always very much behind time in their arrangements; they do not appear yet to understand the value of time—whether in their councils, their daily work, their feasts, or their attendance at church, they are generally behind the appointed hour. If a council is called to commence at noon, three or four Indians will have perhaps assembled at that hour; others straggle in as the day wears on; they sit or lie about, smoking their pipes, chewing tobacco, and talking; and it will probably be three o'clock before the council actually commences.

The Indian feast of to-day was no exception to the rule. It was appointed to take place at noon, but hour after hour sped by, and it was nearly four p.m. when they at length commenced. On entering the room where the feast was laid out, we found two seats arranged for us at the end of the apartment beneath an ornamented canopy decked with cedar boughs, and we were requested to sit down. Then the Chief and Shaukeens (both pagans) stood up, and the Chief made a brief oration to the people, which John Jacobs, a young native, then studying for the ministry at Huron College, interpreted for us. The Chief expressed his pleasure in receiving us among them, and his desire that we should become as one of them by receiving Ojebway names; and then, taking me by the hand, he continued: "The name that I have selected for you is one which we greatly respect and hold in fond remembrance; for it was the name of an old and respected Chief of our tribe who lived many years ago and whose name we wish to have retained; and seeing you are a missionary to the Ojebway Indians, it is the wish of my tribe as well as myself that you should be called after our late respected Chief; so your name hereafter is 'Puhgukahbun' (Clear Day-light)."

The moment my name was given, "Heugh! Heugh!" sounded from all sides, that being the Indian mode of expressing approval when anything is said or done.

Mrs. Wilson then rose and received her name in the same manner. The Chief, addressing her, said: "It is with great pleasure that I bestow also on you, the wife of the missionary, an Ojebway name. The name I am about to give you was the name of one of our sisters who has long since passed away from our midst, and it is our wish that her name should be retained among us. Your name therefore is 'Nahwegeezhegooqua' (Lady of the Sky).

"Heugh! Heugh! Heugh!" again sounded through the room, and then the Indians one and all pressed forward to have a shake of the hand with their new brother and sister. We almost had our hands shaken off, and from all sides came the cry, "Boozhoo, Boozhoo, Puhgukahbun; Boozhoo, Nahwegeezhegooqua, Boozhoo, Boozhoo!"

As soon as order was restored, the feast began. I had the seat of honour next to the Chief, and Mrs. Wilson sat next to me. The table was well covered with eatables—venison, cakes, pork, Indian bread, preserves, all in the greatest abundance. About thirty persons sat down to the first table, the others waiting with true Indian patience for their turn to come; and a long time it was coming, for as soon as the first set had finished, an intermission was made for music and speechifying. Several very pretty songs were sung by the Indian choir, some in English and some in Indian.

After the feast was over and the tables cleared, I was asked to address the people, and Wagimah interpreted for me. I told them briefly how much pleased I was to receive an Ojebway name, and thus become one of their number, and how Mrs. Wilson and myself would now feel that we could shake hands with them and regard them as our brothers and sisters. God, I said, had greatly prospered our work since I came among them. We had already our church completed and our Mission-house nearly so at Sarnia; the great Society in England had contributed five hundred dollars towards the erection of these buildings, and our friends in England about five hundred dollars more; so that there would be no debt. As soon as we had money enough I hoped that with their help we should be able also to build a little church and teacher's house for them here at Kettle Point, and send a catechist to reside among them and teach their children. It was late in the evening when we bade good-bye and drove back to Forest, where we remained for the night and the next morning returned to Sarnia. On our arrival I found a letter awaiting me from the Secretary of the Church Missionary Society, authorizing me to place a catechist in charge of the Kettle Point Mission.

CHAPTER VI.

Christmas on the Reserve.

We were anxious as soon as possible to have both church and Mission-house built on the Sarnia Reserve, so that we might move down among the Indians and dwell in their midst. When therefore the matter of the land was settled, and one acre of Antoine Rodd's farm had been given over for the use of our Mission, we began preparations for the erection of the two buildings. For the building of the church, I wished the Indians to give as much in the way of labour and help as possible, so as to show their earnestness in the cause; but for the erection of the Mission-house, we had to depend largely on contributions from our friends in England. However, the Church Missionary Society made us a grant of £100, and friends helped literally, so that we had no lack of funds, and by the time the two buildings were completed and fenced round with a board fence, all was paid for.

We moved into our new house on the 29th of January, 1869, just six months after our arrival in Canada. It was a nice little frame cottage, with a large room or hall in the centre, study and bed-room on one side, and sitting-room and bed-room on the other; and at the back, connected by a covered passage, were the kitchen and pantry, with servants' bed-room over. We were close to the river, and from our front windows could see in summer-time all the shipping passing to and fro, which made it quite lively.

We were sorry not to get into our Mission-house before Christmas, but this was impossible. Our little church, however, was opened for service two days after Christmas Day, and was beautifully decorated for the occasion.

I must go back a little, and tell how it all happened. I had bought some pews from an old Scotch church in the town which was going to be pulled down, and one day early in December we got them carried down to our little church building, and the Indians assisted me in putting them up; there were ten on each side, and as they would seat five each we had room for a congregation of just a hundred persons. On Christmas Day, thirty-four people assembled in the log-house, which had been beautifully decorated by the Indian women with cedar branches for the occasion. After service I took the opportunity to say something to them about the arrangements in the new church. Among other things I suggested that they should sit together in families instead of the men on one side and the women on the other, as had been their custom. The proposal was well received and caused some amusement. Shesheet said humorously that he would consider it a great privilege to be allowed to sit by his wife. Just as we were coming away the old Chief's wife, Mrs. Chief as we used to call her, came running after Mrs. Wilson with a parcel, and pushed it into her hand, saying in her broken English, "Christmas, Christmas!" It proved to be a prettily worked sweet-grass basket, and the old lady giggled and laughed joyfully as Mrs. Wilson expressed her surprise and pleasure at the present.

Two clergymen besides myself assisted in the services at the opening of the church, which on that occasion was crammed with about a hundred and fifty people. One of the most interesting features was just at the close of the service, when an Indian named Buckwheat, from the neighbouring mission of Walpole Island, came forward, and, after giving a short address expressing the sympathy that was felt by the Walpole Islanders for the Indians of this newly-formed Church mission, proceeded to loosen a belt from his waist, and to take from it a little carefully wrapped up packet, which he brought forward and presented as the offering of his brethren towards the erection of our church and Mission-house. It contained nine dollars.

The next day was the children's treat and Christmas tree. It was held in the hall of the new house, although we had not yet moved in. It was amusing to watch the faces of the children as they gazed upon the unusual sight of a Christmas tree lighted up with tapers. Not even the older people had ever seen one before. There were thirty-one children present, and there was some little gift for each of them. During the evening we taught them to scramble for nuts and candies. It was absurd to see them at first all standing in mute astonishment and wondering at my ruthless waste in throwing away such excellent sweatmeats all over the floor; however, they soon learned how to perform their part of the game, and began scrambling for the good things as eagerly as any English children.

The Indians, although to all appearance so grave and stoical, have a fund of quiet wit and humour about them, and are even sometimes quite boisterous in their merriment. Joseph Wawanosh, the Chief's eldest son, was a particularly quiet grave-looking man, and yet there was often a merry twinkle in his eye, and sometimes he would come out with some funny remark in his quaint broken English. He was our churchwarden, and had a great weakness for making up large fires in the church, to which my wife strongly objected, and they waged a chronic war on the subject. Joseph, when spoken to, used to pretend to shiver, and say he felt particularly cold. One day Mrs. Wilson said to him, "How soon is your wife coming home?" "Oh, about two weeks," he replied. "Why, you will be starved before then; you have no one to cook for you." "Ah, no, I guess not," replied Joe; "Indian never starve in bush." "Why not?" asked Mrs. Wilson. "Oh," said Joe, shaking his head humorously; "lots of squirrels." Old Antoine Rodd, or Shesheet, as he was more generally called, was a huge portly man, and was often very comical in his remarks, his good-natured face beaming with fun. One day Mrs. Wilson nearly slipped into a large puddle while threading her way along the ill-kept road. "What would you have done if I had been drowned?" she asked jokingly, as the old man helped her out of her difficulty. "Oh, I would have dragged it!" he said.

We were very glad when at length we moved

into our new house, and we soon had plenty of our Indian friends to visit us. Widow Kwakegwah brought a black and white cat as a present for my wife. She threw the cat into the kitchen in front of her, and then followed laughing. It was amusing to watch the cat making a survey of the whole house with true Indian curiosity. The Indians did not generally venture beyond the kitchen part without invitation; in that part, however, they made themselves quite at home, and Jane was somewhat taken aback when Joe Wawanosh told her he was going up to see her room. Mrs. Chief also went up, and was delighted with Jane's trunks. She said she would come again another day to see what was in them!

CHAPTER VII.

Mission Work at Sarnia

AFTER settling in at our new home on the Sarnia Reserve, a great part of my time was taken up in exploring through the Bush and visiting the Indians in their houses.

We found one very piteous case of a poor woman in the last stage of consumption. The poor creature was worn to a skeleton lying on a most miserable looking bed with nothing to cover her but a ragged strip of black funereal-looking cloth. Although so very ill, she was able to answer the questions that Wagimah put to her, and when I offered to read the Bible to her she seemed very glad. She listened most attentively while I read in Ojebway the eighteenth chapter of St. Luke, and told her of the love of Christ in coming to save sinners. Then we knelt, and I offered two prayers for the sick copied into my pocket-companion from the Indian prayer-book. We visited the poor creature several times again, and once Mrs. Wilson accompanied me and brought with her some blanc-mange or jelly which she had made. She was much touched at the sight of the poor creature's utter destitution. We were amused as we went along to see a pair of babies' boots hanging on the branch of a tree, evidently placed there by some honest Indian who had chanced to find them on the road. This is what the Indians generally do if they find anything that has been lost,—they hang it up in a conspicuous place, so that the owner may find it again if he comes by the same way.

I had been told of a poor widow who was very ill and living with her three children in a destitute condition. Jane went with me to find her out, and we took a supply of medicine and food with us. After wending our way along a narrow foot-track in the snow, which twisted about among the tall black trees, we came in sight of what looked like a heap of dirty boards and branches of trees piled together, but the blue smoke curling from the top told that it was a human habitation. It was the first time Jane had seen an Indian wigwam, and she was horrified to think that people could live in such a hovel. We drew aside the dirty cloth which covered the entrance and crept in. Two dogs saluted us with snarls, but were soon quieted, and crouching along by the smoky sides of the cabin we shook hands with the poor woman and her daughter (a girl of about fifteen), and then gazed round for something to sit upon;—however, there was nothing but the earthen floor, so down we sat. The little wigwam was just wide enough for a person of ordinary height to lie down in, and in the centre was the fire, so that it may well be imagined that there was not much room to turn round. On one side of the fire lay the poor woman, doubled up in a dirty blanket, for she had not been able to straighten herself for nearly two years, and was quite unable to sit up; another blanket was fastened up against the side of the place to shelter her from the wind. On the other side of the fire crouched the daughter, listening to what I said about administering the medicines. A little boy with bright eyes and a stock of uncombed black hair was also crouching over the fire. This was Willie, the youngest of the family, now about five years old, and little did I think then how much I should have to do with that boy in his after life. Sitting down by the poor woman, I uncovered my basket and displayed my medicines, and explained to the daughter how the mixture was to be taken twice a day, and the liniment to be rubbed on the affected parts. Jane then changed places with me and applied some of the liniment, and the poor creature immediately felt some relief and began talking about it to her daughter. These poor people seemed to be entirely dependent on the kindness of their neighbours; it was old Shesheet who first told me about them, and I understood that he used often to send them food or firewood. When I visited her on another cold day in October, accompanied by my wife, we found her coiled up in her rags moaning with pain, and only a few dying embers to keep her warm. Little Willie was coiled up asleep in a sheepskin. While we stood, Willie roused up out of his nest, and came to see what was going on; his sister, however, motioned him to go back, and, like a discontented little puppy, he made a low sort of whine, and buried himself again, head and all, in his sheepskin. We went back to the Mission-house and brought some tea for the poor woman, which she drank eagerly, and we provided her also with a candle stuck in a bottle and some firewood, but she never smiled, or said thank you. Her feelings as well as her features seemed to have become hardened with constant pain and suffering. However, we were agreeably surprised one day when she presented my wife with four tiny baskets, tastefully made, and a smile for once actually played on her lips. Some time after she was taken into a house by some friendly Indians, and kindly cared for, the result of which was that she became gradually better.

Very soon after our arrival at Sarnia we had proposed to the Indian women that they should meet together once a week for needlework and reading, but the scheme was not carried into effect until we had settled in our new house on the Reserve. The first meeting was held in our hall in the summer of 1869. On the hall-table were spread out all the articles of clothing sent to us from England, and we had on view patterns of prints, flannels, &c., from one of the dry goods stores in the town, the prices being affixed, and discount allowed at ten per cent.

As soon as all were assembled I explained to them that the object in meeting together was that they might provide clothing for themselves and their children at as cheap a rate as possible, and at the same time might have an opportunity for friendly talk and instruction. The plan would be for them to engage in needlework for an hour and a half, during part of which time I would read to them a story, which my interpreter had translated into Indian, and after that we would have scripture reading, singing, and prayer to close the meeting. After all who wished to become members of the meeting had given me their names, they were invited to inspect the patterns and select the material with which they wished to make a beginning. We found the plan answer very well, and soon our "Mothers' Meeting" was thoroughly established.

But it was not always that everything went on so harmoniously and peacefully. Unhappily there was a considerable amount of whiskey-drinking among the men, and sometimes drunken fights would occur in close proximity to the house. A son of Antoine Rodd's was particularly vicious when under the influence of liquor; once he frightened us all by making a murderous attack on his father with his tomahawk and gun, and the old man had to escape back into the Bush for his life. Another time the wife of this same man came rushing into our house with her infant on her breast and another daughter following,—her drunken husband running after and threatening to kill them. We dragged them in and shut and locked all the doors, and soon the man was pounding away and trying to get in. The two women in great alarm locked themselves up in the pantry and remained all night under our protection. The saddest occurrence of all was when a man named Winter was actually killed by his own son while in a state of intoxication. We did what we could to try and stem the tide of drunkenness by forming a Temperance Society, which a large number of the

Indians joined; but a more effectual check has of late years been put upon the terrible practice by the action of the Dominion Government; it is now against law for a white man either to give or sell liquor to an Indian on any pretence, and the penalty is very heavy.

I must finish this chapter with an account of an Indian funeral. The daughter of one of our Indians, named Kwakejewun, had fallen sick and died—died, as we hoped, trusting in her Saviour. As is usual among the Indians, a large number of people gathered together to show their sympathy with the bereaved parents, and to follow the body to the grave. The coffin was first brought into the church. I read the usual service, and a hymn was sung very sweetly and plaintively. Then we proceeded to the cemetery, nearly a mile distant. The snow was deep on the ground and sparkling in the sunlight. I drove in my cutter and headed the long funeral procession. A sad and picturesque sight it was; from eighty to a hundred people in all, some in sleighs, some ploding through the snow on foot,—aged women in their white blankets, mothers with their children, some of them in bright scarlet shawls, boys and girls, all in their Sunday attire. Through the silent forest we wended our way till we came at length to the wild little cemetery with its rude snake fence encircling it. The coffin was taken from the sleigh and carefully lowered into the grave; then the men took off their hats and we sang another hymn. It sounded very sweet in that wild desolate spot, and the poor mother stood enveloped in a blanket at the head of the open grave, and, with her eyes fixed on her daughter's coffin, joined in the singing. Then I read the remainder of the service, and, having shaken hands with the poor father and mother, returned home. The mother grasped my hand warmly, and met me with a happy smile. She believed, I think, that her child was safe with the Saviour.

CHAPTER VIII.

The Bishop's Visit.

WE were now well settled into our Indian home at Sarnia, and my work was clearly defined. The Sarnia Reserve was our head-quarters. Here there were some 400 Indians, and at Kettle Point, thirty miles away, were about 100 more. The out-stations were to be New Credit, Saugeen, and Cape Croker, which places together contained about 1150 Indians. The idea was to place a catechist at each of these distant settlements, and for me to visit them twice or three times in the year. With the view of providing catechists suitable for the work I was authorized by the Church Missionary Society to receive and educate some young men; and within a few months after we had taken up our residence on the Reserve I commenced to teach two young Indians, named Wilson Jacobs and William Henry, with the view of their becoming catechists.

The great event of the summer was a visit we received from the Bishop of Huron and Mrs. Cronyn. The fact that twenty-five persons were confirmed, and that forty-five came forward afterwards to receive the Holy Communion, will show that our work among these poor Indians had already made some progress. Among the candidates for confirmation was poor old Quasind, who came up bare-footed, a great-grandfather, and, I suppose, about ninety years of age. In the evening our own child, Archibald Edward, was christened during the time of Divine service by the Bishop.

The following day we had appointed to have a gathering of Indians, a sort of social party, to meet the Bishop. When morning broke, however, rain was pouring in torrents, and a picnic on the grass became altogether out of the question. So, after early dinner, our hall was cleared, and the business of cutting up bread-and-butter and cake and preparing the tea began. Two or three Indian women had made their appearance, and were soon hard at work with merry faces and busy hands. About 6 p.m. the Indians began to arrive, and by half-past seven sixty had collected. Tea being ready, we called in as many as we could pack into our hall; others sat in the passage or on cordwood piles outside; then each had a cup and saucer given him, and baskets full of bread-and-butter, buns, and cake, and tea were carried round, and all ate their fill.

The hall table was covered with books, illustrated magazines, maps, &c., and as soon as the Indians had finished tea they took up these and amused themselves with the pictures. There was a draught-board also, which engrossed the attention of some of the young men, many of them being very clever in playing the game. An old Indian, generally known as "the Doctor," caused great merriment by singing one or two old Indian songs in that peculiar tone of voice which only an Indian can command. The great event of the evening was the conferring of an Indian name on our little boy, only a few months old. The task was delegated to old Shesheet. The old man came forward with his usual radiant face, and after a few prefatory remarks, expressing his great pleasure in meeting the Bishop and Mrs. Cronyn, he took "the pale-faced babe" into his arms and conferred upon it the name of "Tecumseh," a great warrior who many years ago fell in battle fighting under the British flag. After I had thanked the Indians for making my little boy one of themselves, the Bishop rose and gave a very nice address, which Waginah interpreted. He told them how anxious he had been to see these, his Indian brothers and sisters, ever since he had heard of their becoming members of the Church of their great mother the Queen. He was very pleased indeed to see them, and so was his "squaw," who had come with him, and he wished them every prosperity and happiness and the blessing of God on the Mission. Before parting we sang a hymn, and then closed with prayer and the blessing. The Bishop and Mrs. Cronyn stood up at the end of the hall and shook hands with the Indians one by one as they passed out.

In accordance with the instructions I had received from the C.M.S., I made arrangements as soon as practicable for placing a catechist in charge of the Kettle Point Mission, and about this time gave up employing an interpreter, as his services would be no longer needed, and I had now a good stock of sermons written in Indian which I could use at my Sunday services. Before long, John Jacobs, the young native student already mentioned, and who, after satisfactorily passing his course at the Theological College, was ordained in July 1869, took up his abode at Kettle Point as my assistant Missionary. Besides preaching on the Sunday, he taught school during the week, so that his time was well occupied.

It was just about this time that I had a severe attack of fever, which for the time quite prostrated me, and my medical adviser ordered me to go away for a few weeks' rest and change of air. So Mr. Jacobs came to take my place at Sarnia and with two of his sisters occupied the Mission-house during our absence. After spending a week with friends in Toronto, we thought we would explore a more northern region, and visit Mr. Chance's Mission at Garden River, which we had often heard of, so we took train to Collingwood, and were soon on our way up the lakes in the beautiful steamboat *Chicora*.

Thus was God gradually opening the way for us, and preparing for us a larger and more important sphere of work.

It was on this visit to Garden River that I first felt drawn in spirit towards the Indians of the Lake Superior region, that there first entered into my mind the idea of an institution for training the young Indians, and that I first made the acquaintance of the old Indian chief, Augustin Shingwauk.

CHAPTER IX.

First Visit to Garden River.

We met with a hearty welcome from Mr. and Mrs. Chance, though we had never seen them before. Their church and Mission-house and little log school-house were picturesquely situated on rising ground quite close to the river. The Mission-house, which occupied the centre of the three buildings, was constructed of logs clapboarded over and whitewashed. It had a verandah in front, over the trellis work of which hops grew in profusion, and clambered upwards to the roof. In front of the house was a neat little garden, with two or three fir-trees, some lilac bushes, and well-filled flower-beds. There was quite a profusion of roses, which, even at this late season of the year, scented the air deliciously. Outside the garden fence, with its green gate, was a field of Indian corn which sloped down almost to the water's edge. The view from the steps of the verandah was very pretty; one could see the broad deep St. Maria River, nearly a mile wide, and long lines of sailing vessels towed by small tugs, occasionally passing and repassing on their way from the upper to the lower lakes. Across the river were the well-wooded hills of Sugar Island, with here and there a settler's shanty and clearing. To the left hand could still be seen the broad river winding its course down toward Lake George, the smaller stream, called Garden River, joining it a short distance below. Then behind, the scene was equally, if not more grand—high rocky hills scantily clad with fir and birch-trees. We felt that we were now indeed in the land of the Indian, far away from civilization; no railways, no telegraphs, no omnibuses or street cars, no hotels or shops for many hundred miles.

There was something very attractive and fascinating about this first visit to the wilds of Algoma. We were entertained royally. Peaches, cream, and preserved fruits were among the dainties which covered the table. Where all the good things came from was a matter of wonder to us. The meat, however, consisting of a hind quarter of mutton, had, we found, come with us on the boat, and it just lasted out our four days' visit. We were told extraordinary stories about the difficulty of procuring the necessaries of life, and the manner of overcoming difficulties. Until quite lately the steamboats in their passage up the lakes had never deigned to stop at Garden River; now, however, through Mr. Chance's exertions, a dock had been made and a Post-office erected; and about once in ten days a steam vessel would stop to leave or receive the mails. Mr. and Mrs. Chance were Postmaster and Post-mistress, and we had many a joke with them on the subject. Their fresh meat was always procured from the steamboats. Before this new arrangement was made, the steward on the boat used to tie the meat to a log of wood, and haul it overboard opposite the Mission-house, and Mr. Chance had to go out in his boat to pick it up. They had a capital large sail boat, with two sails, called *The Missionary*. It had lately been presented to the Mission by the Cathedral Sunday School, Toronto. It was very interesting to meet with the Indians of this locality. Many of them were tall, fine-looking men; notably so Augustin Shingwauk and Buhkwujjenene, both of them Chiefs, and very intelligent-looking men. Augustin was at this time about 60 years of age, and his brother Buhkwujjenene eight or ten years his junior. They could trace their ancestry back for four generations. Their father's name was Shingwaukoons (Little Pine), and he appears, from all accounts, to have been a very intelligent Chief. The father of Shingwaukoons was partly French, but his mother, Ogemahqua (Queen), was pure Indian, and daughter of a Chief named Shingahbawuhsin, and this Chief again was son of a Chief named Tuhgwahna, all of them residents of the Sault Ste. Marie district.

The Indians of Garden River were not nearly so far advanced in civilization as those of Sarnia; very little was done in the way of cultivating the soil, and very few of them could speak any English. They, however, seemed to evince great interest in religion, the services were well attended, the responses in the Indian tongue well made, and the singing hearty.

I must relate one sad incident that occurred during our short visit. It was a beautiful Sunday towards the end of September; we had had service in the white frame church, and very attentive and orderly had the congregation been while Mr. Chance read the service and interpreted my preaching. I had been speaking on the subject of "Eternal Life" —"This is life eternal, that they might know Thee, the only True God, and Jesus Christ whom Thou hast sent." Very wrapt was the attention as I endeavoured to unfold before my simple hearers the great and wondrous subject of eternal life. Had they—sitting there before me—anything to do with this eternal life? Perhaps their thoughts day by day were on the things of this world—their fishing, their hunting, their basket-making, or planting or digging potatoes. Did they ever think that they had souls to be saved; that before another Sunday came round these things which now took up their time and thoughts might have passed away for ever, and they themselves have entered upon the eternal state? If they were true Christians, they would then be meeting with God, beholding Him face to face; they would be with the holy angels, with Jesus. But if not prepared, where would they be? A great gulf would be between them and heaven—a great impassable gulf; they would be with the lost! Before another Sunday came round this great and wonderful change might take place. Were they prepared?

Among my hearers were two women; one on the left hand side of the church was a newly-married young woman wearing a scarlet shawl and a hat with flowers. She could not have been more than twenty. The other, who was her mother, sat on the opposite side; an old woman—a widow—wrapped in a black shawl. The husband of the young woman was in the gallery overhead.

Service was over, and we had wended our way back to the parsonage, followed by several Indians, men and women with their babes, who had come to shake hands or to ask for "muskeke" (medicine). All at once we heard a shout from the garden, and a girl came rushing up, crying: "Quick! help! there are people drowning." We all ran off with great haste to the shore, the Indian women wailing in their own peculiar way, some burying their heads in their shawls and sobbing with grief. Quite a little fleet of boats and canoes were already off to the rescue; six or seven in all. We could not at first make out where was the scene of the disaster, but soon it became only too apparent. There, far out in the very centre of the broad river, being carried away by the current, were four or five specks, the heads of people struggling to save themselves. The boats were still a long distance from them, and breathlessly we watched as they made their way onward. Two, three of the specks had disappeared; only two were now visible. "How many were in the boat?" was anxiously asked. "Oh, there must have been eight or nine;" and only two now above water. It was sickening to think of. The wailing cries of the women on the shore increased each moment, and great was the suspense as the foremost boat drew with all speed towards the poor drowning creatures. I waited to see the two who were afloat pulled into the boats, and then hurried up to the house to see if all needful preparations had been made. Mrs. Chance had got everything ready; a good bright fire, blankets, and brandy. When I went back to the shore, the poor half-drowned creatures had just landed. Shaking and shivering they were lifted out of the boat and supported up to the house. Four had been saved: two men and two women. One was still missing, the young wife who had worn the hat and flowers! The children who were supposed to have gone, it was found on inquiry had been providentially left behind. As soon as we could get the poor creatures up to the house, we set to work to revive them.

One of the men, the husband of her who had not yet been found, was on the point of giving in when the boat reached him, and in a moment more would probably have sunk. He was perfectly cold when we brought him in, and being in a consumptive state at the time of his immersion, we much feared that he would not survive the shock. The poor old woman's heart seemed almost broken at the loss of her daughter, and she sat wailing in the kitchen the whole afternoon. The house was of course crowded with Indians who came in to help or sympathize. From those who went to the rescue we learned that the poor woman who was drowned had her hand above the water when the boat came up, but she sank before the people could seize it. Her hat was afterwards found about two miles below the place where she sank. In the evening the poor old woman described how the accident had happened. She said the boat was small and rather too heavily-laden. Just as they got to the middle of the river, a breeze sprang up, and the waves began coming over the side. One of the men jumped into the water to lighten it, but it was of no use. The boat filled, and in a few moments they were all struggling in the water. The poor old creature described how she sank to a great depth, and then rose again; how she prayed to Kezha-Musnedoo (the Good Spirit) to save her; how she sank again; and then, while under the water, saw the dark shadow of the boat coming over her; how again she rose to the surface and was saved.

We met again for service in the evening, and Mr. Chance preached very solemnly to a large congregation from the words, " Prepare to meet thy God."

A day or two after this we left the Garden River Mission and returned to Sarnia.

CHAPTER X.

Baptism of Pagans.

There were not many genuine Pagans either at Sarnia or at Kettle Point. Pagan practices had fallen altogether into disuse. There were some Indians living who had been "medicine men," but

we never heard that they practised their charms. Still there were several families who held aloof from Christianity. When spoken to about being baptized, their reply was that they thought the Christian Indians behaved worse than the Pagan Indians, and they were afraid that if they were baptized they would become as bad. It was sad that such a thing could be said, and sadder still that there should be any truth about it. Of course the mere fact of the Indians being brought into contact with white people would lead them into temptations from which, in their wild wandering state, they had been comparatively free. It has been said even by white travellers that they have found the pagan Indians of the North more honest and trustworthy than those in a semi-civilized and nominally Christian state. The Indian when he mixes with the Whites soon learns their bad habits, but is more slow to learn what is holy and good.

There were several families at Kettle Point who at the time when we established our Mission were still nominally Pagan. Chief among them were Ahbettuhwahnuhgund and his sister, and Shaukeens, with his wife and family. Ahbettuhwahnuhgund's wife had been baptized, and so also had his two eldest children. One of the first religious rites that I was asked to perform when I began to visit Kettle Point was to receive into the Christian fold the Chief's little boy and aged sister; and at the same time the wife of Shaukeens, who had had several rather dangerous attacks of illness, was baptized. We called the little boy Cornelius, and Mrs. Shaukeens received the name of Tabitha.

It was strange how superstitious the Indians continued to be even after their acceptance of Christianity. They seemed never to lose altogether their faith in witchcraft, especially in that form by which it was believed that certain persons had power to cause sickness or misfortune to others. They seemed also to have a firm belief in dreams. Once I was visiting at a poor miserable little shanty on the Sarnia Reserve, and found an old man and his son both lying very sick. The poor creatures were in a wretched condition, the hovel they were in consisting merely of strips of bark and old boards outside and inside hung with rags and tatters and old cloths of every description. The only person to tend them was an old woman—wife, I suppose, of the elder man—who was crouching over the fire smoking her pipe. When we came in, the sick man was gnawing a duck bone, some one having shot him a wild duck. He said it was the first time he had eaten anything for several days; his son was too ill to eat anything. The old man told Wagimah that he had seen me before, a night or two ago in a dream. I had made a garden, and divided it into four parts, and one of these parts was very miserable and wretched. I was walking through this miserable part one day, when I found this poor man. He was very sick indeed, and I took him up and brought him into another part of the garden which was very beautiful, and told him that he might stay there and work, and be happy for ever. Such was his dream. I repeated some verses of Scripture to the poor creature, and then we knelt and prayed. I heard afterwards that the people around believed the old man to be bewitched; some evilly-disposed " medicine man," they said, had brought this sickness upon him by his enchantments.

It was a very interesting occasion when the whole of Shaukeens' family, consisting of seven children, were brought to me for baptism.

At 2 p.m. the horn was blown, and the people began to come together to our little temporary school-house. About twenty-eight assembled, and we began service with a hymn; then I read the evening prayers from my Ojebway prayer-book, and at the close of the lesson began the baptismal service. David Sahpah, his wife, and Adam stood sponsors for the children. The names given to them were Stephen, Emma, Sutton, Esther, Alice, Talfourd, and Wesley. Before their baptism, they had no names, and I had to register them in my book as No. 1 boy, No. 2 girl, and so on. It was curious to notice how Pagans attending our services never made any change in their position as the service proceeded. This time the mother, who had been baptized about two months before, kneeled, or stood, or sat with the other people; but the father and children sat quietly on their seats. After the service the children joined in the devotions, and the father only remained sitting.

The Chief Ahbettuhwahnuhgund for a long time refused to be baptized, although I very often had conversations with him on the subject, and I felt that in his heart he fully believed the great truths of Christianity. It was partly, perhaps, pride that kept him back, and partly that he was waiting, as he said, to see the Church of England Mission firmly established at Kettle Point.

In the first week of January, 1870, our new school-church and master's house at Kettle Point were opened for use. Very pretty they looked as we approached; three flags were flying, and there were crowds of Indians around. Mr. Jacobs, who was now settled in charge of the Mission, met us on the steps of the little church, and accompanied us in. It was most tastefully decorated, and fitted up with a reading-desk on each side, dark-stained communion rails, and crimson coverings. Forty-five persons assembled at the opening service, and just filled the seats. It was a cause of much satisfaction to the Indians to have their little church, which they had worked so hard to build, at length completed. They had themselves supplied all the saw-logs out of which the lumber was made, and had put up the framework, so that it had been but a very small expense to the Mission.

Shortly after this I received word from the Chief that he was anxious to be baptized. His answer to my questions were very simple and childlike, and I had every reason to hope that he was sincere in his desire to be a Christian. "Many of these things that you tell me," he said, "are new to me. I hear them now for the first time; nevertheless, I believe them. I believe all that the Christian's book teaches; I cannot but believe it. No man could have written that book. I receive it all as true, and I trust that I may gradually learn all that there is to be learnt about the Christian religion."

I gave him the name of Isaac, that being a name by which he had been commonly known among the white people for some time past. It was very interesting to kneel with that newly-baptized Indian Chief, and hear him for the first time pronounce those sacred words, "Wayoosemegooyun Kezhegoong ayahyun"—"Thou who art our Father, in heaven who art." The Chief, his wife, his sister, and his children were all now Christians, and could unite together in prayer and praise and Christian worship.

CHAPTER XI.

The Red River Expedition.

The year 1870 was memorable in Europe for the great war between France and Germany, followed by the loss of the Pope's temporal power, and the establishment of secular government in Rome. Here in Canada the excitement of the day was the Red River rebellion, to quell which a military expedition was despatched under the command of General (then Colonel) Wolseley. I had arranged to make a Missionary tour to Lake Superior during the summer, and it so happened that I fell in with the troops on their way up the lake and did service for them as chaplain while they were encamped at Thunder Bay.

It was a busy scene in the dock at Collingwood just prior to starting. There were about a hundred Iroquois Indians who had been engaged as guides and boatmen, and these were to precede the expedition and arrange for the portaging and crossing the rivers before the arrival of the troops. The steamship *Chicora* was moored to the dock, the whole vessel from stem to stern being heavily laded down, and there was considerable delay before we started, but at length the ropes were let go, the planks drawn in, and we were off. This was the *Chicora's* first trip of the season, and large crowds gathered about the docks at the various places where we stopped on our way up the lakes, the general expectation evidently being that the troops would be on board. The disappointment was great when it was found that we had only an advanced guard of Indian Voyageurs with us. One old lady, accosting one of the passengers, in her enthusiasm exclaimed, "Have ye got the army on board?" Above Manitoulin Island the channel becomes very narrow and is sprinkled with little rocky islets clad scantily with fir and birch trees. On one was living an old grey haired man in charge of a lighthouse; he had been there the whole winter shut in by ice and snow, and was so full of delight at witnessing "the first boat of the season" that he saluted us by firing his gun, to which we responded by a grunting whistle. At last we reached Garden River, and stepping on shore, I was soon exchanging hearty greetings with Mr. and Mrs. Chance. The *Chicora* was detained four hours at this place, as all the boats for the expedition were to be taken off before they proceeded further and to be rowed by the Indians to Sault Ste. Marie, a distance of twelve miles. It was necessary to do this because the only way for the *Chicora* to get into Lake Superior was through a canal on the American side of the river, and if the boats were left on board they might be regarded by the American Government as munitions of war and so be refused passage. So the Indians were to take charge of the boats and pole them up the rapids, while the *Chicora* expected to go innocently through the locks as a boat of peace. However the plan did not answer; the *Chicora* even though divested of her boats, was refused passage, and having unloaded everything on the Canadian side was obliged to return whence she came. Then a road had to be cut along the Canadian shore, the red-wheeled waggons brought into use, and everything conveyed a distance of some three miles to a point above the rapids, where a dock was constructed and another Canadian vessel, the *Algoma* employed to carry the things on to Thunder Bay on the shore of Lake Superior.

As there was likely under these circumstances to be considerable delay before I could continue my journey, I passed my leisure time under the hospitable roof of Mr. and Mrs. Chance, and was glad of the opportunity to renew my acquaintance with the Indians whom we had met last fall. I had hoped that Mr. Chance would have been able to accompany me on my expedition up the Lake; indeed it had been his own wish to do so, and in that case we should have taken his own boat *The Missionary* and a crew of Indians, and so have been independent of the steamboats. Circumstances however occurred to prevent the carrying out of this plan, and in the end I started alone by steamboat, with my tent, camp-bed, a good stock of books, provisions, &c., and a Garden River Indian named James as my attendant. Col. Wolseley and his staff and a large detachment of troops were on board the steamboat, and on arrival at Thunder Bay, about 300 miles distant from Sault Ste. Marie, we found a scene of the greatest activity and excitement. The troops, about 1200 in number, were encamped on a wild bare spot with only a few rough shanties and houses, about three miles from the Hudson Bay Company Post, Fort William. The Bush had been burnt over, and it was a most desolate, uninviting looking place, although the distant scenery around was grand. There was considerable difficulty in disembarking, as the water near the shore was shallow and there was no dock, so everything had to be taken from the steamboat to the land in a flat scow hauled to and fro by a rope. We pitched our tent on the shore, close to the soldiers' camp, other tents of explorers and travellers being close around us. From this point the troops were to start on their journey to Winnipeg. First, forty miles of road had to be constructed, and boats and everything had to be carried on waggons till the first water in the chain of lakes and rivers was reached. This had to be done for the whole of the 700 miles to Winnipeg; wherever possible the troops went by boat, and where there was no water on the route, a road had to be constructed and the waggons used. It was no easy task that Colonel Wolseley had before him in this wild, uninhabited and rocky country.

Very soon after my arrival at Thunder Bay I began to look about for Indians, that being the primary object of my visit. I found quite a large settlement of them at Fort William, but was disappointed to discover that they were all Roman Catholics. The Jesuits, it appeared, had been among them for more than a century. They had a priest resident among them, an old man, I was told, gentlemanly, courteous, and generally beloved and respected both by Indians and Whites; they had also a little church decorated with flowers and images. However, I managed to draw a few people around me, and scarcely a day passed but I had Indian visitors to my tent. The Indian Chief, whose name was Mungedenah, did not seem to be at all bigoted in his religion. Pointing to the sky, he said, "I know there is only one God, and I do not think Christians ought to be divided." He seemed most anxious to have an Ojebway Testament. I told him that the Garden River Indians could nearly all read the Testament for themselves. Tears came into his eyes, and he said he wished indeed it could be the same with them. When he rose to leave, he thanked me, and pointing up to heaven said God would bless me.

After the visit of their Chief the Indians got quite friendly, and used often to come and see me in my tent. One of them remarked once that he thought there must be a great many white people in the world, to judge by the large number that had come together that summer in such a short space of time. Some of the poor creatures were evidently afraid of being reported to their priest when they came to visit me; they generally squatted at the entrance of the tent, and appeared to be keeping a watch all the time, so that it was very seldom that I had an opportunity of reading to them. Perhaps the most interesting incident that occurred was an interview that I had with some wild pagan Indians from the Interior. Some one put his head in at my tent door, and said, " Have you seen the Indian Chief from Rainy Lake?" "No," I replied, "where is he to be found? I should like very much to see him." Indeed I was most anxious to meet some Indian from that quarter, as I had heard that there was a large settlement there of some thousand Ojebway Indians all in the darkness of paganism. I was directed to a store where the Chief had gone in, and immediately went in search of him. There he stood, a fine, upright, muscular man, with sharp set features, and a fierce forbidding eye; long shaggy black hair straggled down his back, a mink-skin turban graced his forehead, into which were stuck four white eagle feathers, and behind it hung an otter skin appendage like a great bag, and covered with little pieces of bone or metal, which rattled as he walked. I addressed the Chief in Indian, and he turned and shook hands with me, and after a little conversation he agreed to accompany me to my tent, where I prepared a meal for him. He was very ready to converse, and told me that his name was "Makuhda-uhsin" (Black Stone), that he had arrived at Midday, that he was accompanied by four other men, two boys, and a woman, that they had come by canoe, and had camped six nights on the way. Koojeching, he said, was the place where they had come from, and there he had left a thousand warriors.

While he was talking, the rest of the party arrived, seeking their Chief. They all squatted down, and I had to feed them all, and then give them tobacco for a smoke. They were all wild-looking creatures, their countenances as thoroughly unchristianlike as could be conceived. As soon as their hunger was satiated, and they had filled their pipes, they were rising to go, but I asked them to remain as I had a few words still to say to them. I then told them briefly who I was, where I had come from, and my object in coming to Thunder Bay. I had heard, I said, that they were all pagans at Koojeching. I was very sorry for it, and very anxious that they should embrace Christianity. A change came upon their faces as I spoke; they shuffled uneasily, eyed me suspiciously, and were evidently impatient to get away. They probably thought that I had got them into my tent with the idea of using some enchantments or exercising some witchcraft upon them. I did not understand all they said, but James told me afterwards that they were all very angry. They said they were all pagans, and intended to remain so. When I asked whether, if I were to visit them some day, they would listen to me, and if they would like me to come to see them and tell them about God, Black Stone replied, "Come if you will, but as for my people they will never become Christians." I heard afterwards that a Jesuit priest once visited their settlement, and after he had left the small-pox broke out. In their superstitious ignorance, they attributed the disease to the priest's visit, and so determined never to accept Christianity.

I had arranged to visit the Lake Neepigon Indians on my way back down the Lake, and took my

passage on board a steamboat which was to call at Red Rock at the mouth of the Neepigon River. But my purposes were frustrated; the steamboats were under the direction of the military authorities, orders were changed at the last moment, and instead of Red Rock I found myself at Michipicotun. At this place there is a Hudson Bay Company Post, and a small settlement of Indians. The approach to the Post is very picturesque, the river being bordered by high-wooded banks, and the clean-looking white-washed buildings of the Company presented a striking contrast to the wild scenery around as we approached, rowing up the river in one of the ship's boats. We pitched our tent in a cleared spot just across the river, opposite to the Post and near to some Indian wigwams. During our stay, which lasted about ten days, I visited every day among the people, and at nightfall we would meet together in one of their wigwams for reading the Scripture and prayer. The name of the Chief was Tootoomenaun; he lived like the rest of his people in a simple wigwam made of a circle of sticks sloping to a point, and covered with birch-bark; and there, with his family and his dogs, he lay by the fire and smoked his pipe, while I read or talked to them, the smoke circulating about our heads and then finding its escape among the blackened pole-ends at the apex of the little domicile. Another Chief from the neighbouring settlement of Batchee-wanig, about 90 miles distant, was on a visit, and I had many a long talk with these two red-skinned brethren. They said they had had no minister to visit them, either Jesuit or Protestant, since the previous summer, and they seemed very anxious to be taught, and listened very attentively when I read or expounded the Scriptures. Finding the people all so anxious to learn, I opened a little day-school in the Chief's wigwam. I had a box for my seat, and the young people squatted round on mats. There was an attendance of eleven scholars. Two of the young men I found already knew the alphabet, so I set them on to commence the first book while the others were kept busy with the A, B, C. They were sharp at learning, and nearly all of them, with the exception of one or two of the youngest children, knew the capital letters and figures from 1 to 10 by the time the two hours of study were over. This school teaching was continued every day until the steamboat arrived which was to take us the remainder of our homeward voyage to the Sault.

It is interesting to me to recall this, my first missionary visit to Lake Superior. Certainly it did not seem that much was accomplished during my tour, and I was a little disappointed that there was not a larger number of pagan Indians among whom I might look forward to establish Missions in the future. Still I had gained, at any rate, some insight into the condition of the people; there were the obdurate pagans from Rainy Lake, Blackstone, whom I was destined to meet again at a future day, the Thunder Bay Indians all seemingly under Jesuit influence; then these more accessible Red men of Michipicotun and Batcheewanig. Some Pic River Indians also I had chanced to meet on my travels, and had some conversation with. The Neepigon Indians I was sorry to miss seeing. I was obliged to leave them for another time, together with the people belonging to several other settlements on the North shore.

Altogether, the result of my trips to Garden River and to Lake Superior was that I felt inwardly drawn to come and labour among the people of these more Northern regions in preference to remaining among the semi-civilized Indians of Sarnia. How the way would open I could not at that time foresee, or how soon it might be my lot to move into these wilder regions I could not tell. It was merely an unshaped thought, the beginning of a desire created in my breast.

CHAPTER XII.

Changes in Prospect.

It was at the end of June that I arrived at Sarnia. Very glad was I to be at home again after my long, rough journey, and very glad too was my wife to see me, for it was but seldom that we had had an opportunity of writing to one another during my absence. In the autumn our second child was born—a boy—to whom the Indians gave the name of Suhyahquahdung (proclaimer), and shortly after this we gave up our cottage on the Indian Reserve to Mr. Jacobs, and moved to a larger house in the town, where we should have room to take two or three Indian pupils as boarders. This seemed to be a judicious step, as of all things it appeared to be the most important, to commence preparing young men who might afterwards act as catechists and school teachers among their people.

And so Mr. Jacobs, who had recently married, settled in at the Mission-house as Pastor of the Sarnia Indians, and an Indian from Walpole Island was appointed to take his place as catechist at Kettle Point.

Our readers will not have forgotten poor Shegaugooqua, the poor decrepid bed-ridden creature whom we found in such a pitiable condition in an old wigwam back in the Bush. They will remember also the mention we made of her little five-year-old boy, with his shock of rough, black uncombed hair, and his bright intelligent eyes. This little boy, Willie by name, we now took in hand. I arranged that the catechist who had been appointed to the

Kettle Point Mission should take two little boys into his family, and train them up to a Christian and useful life. One of them was to be Willie, and the other a grandchild of the unfortunate man who was murdered—Tommy Winter. So, a few days before Joshua Greenbird was expected, we brought Willie and Tommy to our house in Sarnia to prepare them for entering upon their new life. The first thing was to divest them of their dirty rags, and give them each a thorough good scrubbing; then they were put into two new little suits of grey cloth which my wife and I had each taken a share in making with the sewing machine. Thus, clean and neat, these two little fellows of six years old were shipped off to their new home. Walpole Island, where Joshua the catechist was coming from, was some 40 miles south of Sarnia, and Kettle Point was 30 miles or more to the north, the road lying direct through the town; and as Joshua had arranged to drive in a waggon the whole way with his family and baggage, he made our house his stopping-place on the road, and we gave him and his wife and four children all a lodging for the night; then in the morning they started on again, taking Willie and Tommy with them. For the first week or two the two little boys were quite happy and contented in their new home, and went regularly to school with the other children who lived at Kettle Point; but after a time they got home-sick, and then they did what Indian boys often do when first taken in hand and put under restrictions—they ran away. However, they did not get far on their thirty mile journey homeward before they were accosted by a farmer who was driving along in his waggon. Willie, always ready with his tongue, and already knowing a little English, called to the farmer, "Say, you going Sarnia?" The farmer immediately guessed what was in the wind, and cried, "Yes, come along, boys; jump in." So in they jumped; but were somewhat mortified—poor little fellows—to find themselves, half an hour later, back again at the catechist's house. The lesson was a good one for them, and from that day forward they had the impression deeply printed on their minds that farmers were everywhere on the watch for them, ready to bring them home if they tried to run away.

It was during this winter (1870-71) that we began making plans for building a church for the Sarnia Indians. The little building that we had put up on our first arrival had never been intended as a permanent church; so now that the Mission was fairly established and was beginning to show good signs of prospering, it seemed to be only right that a more substantial building should be erected for the purpose of Divine worship, and that the little frame building should be kept simply for a school. The first thing was to trundle the old building out of the way; so a "bee" was called, and a number of the Indians assembled, and with levers and rollers, and after working hard for a couple of days, the school was twisted round and removed to the far corner of the lot. Then the foundations were dug for the new church. It was decided that it should be a brick building, with a spire, to cost about 1500 dollars. Mr. Jacobs, my assistant, busied himself in the matter, and together we managed to raise the requisite funds; and early in the spring building operations were commenced.

However, it was not my destiny to be the pastor of this little brick church among the Sarnia Indians. God was calling me to other work. It so happened that, in the providence of God, the Garden River Mission just at this time fell vacant. The Rev. Mr. Chance, who had laboured there so faithfully for the past 18 years, was called away to another sphere in a more southerly district. Great were the lamentations of the poor Garden River Indians when he left. Both he and his wife had become much endeared to the people. Mrs. Chance was the schoolmistress and doctor, and what would the poor children and the poor sick people do without her? and what would they do without their Missionary who had laboured so long and so faithfully among them: who had baptized their children, and united their young people in marriage, and buried their dead, and preached to them the glad tidings of the Gospel, and visited them, and sympathized with them, and helped them in their homes? Mr. Chance's children had all been born and brought up at Garden River; Indian nurses had attended them and cared for them during their infant days; the Indian women had learned to look upon them almost as their own; and one dear little girl—Alice—had died after a short illness, and was buried in the Indian Cemetery. It was a terrible wrench for these poor Indians one and all to be separated from their Missionary and his family. And the worst feature of all was that there seemed to be considerable fear lest the Mission might be given up altogether. The New England Company, under whose auspices Mr. Chance had worked, had determined on withdrawing from that portion of the field; and unless some other Society saw fit to take them up, there seemed but little prospect that the work among them would be continued.

All these things weighed with me, and I earnestly sought the guidance of Almighty God in prayer, content to follow His will and to be led by His hand.

As Mr. Chance intended to leave Garden River early in the spring, and it was a part of my duty to make extended tours among the scattered Indians, and minister to their spiritual wants, I decided on making another trip northward as soon as possible after navigation opened. My wife accompanied me, and we took an Indian boy with us, named Aleck Bird, as cook and general servant.

CHAPTER XIII.

Roughing it.

WE expected that when we got to Garden River we should find an empty house, and have to do everything for ourselves; so we came well provided with a supply of flour, salt meat, &c., &c. Quite a crowd of Indians came running down to the dock when we landed, and all were eager to shake hands, crying, "Boozhoo, boozhoo," the Indian mode of address. Then one seized a bundle, another a portmanteau, and, all laden with our baggage and supplies, accompanied us up to the Mission-house. Chief Buhkwujjenene was most warm in his greetings. "Would that you could always remain with us!" he exclaimed. On arriving at the little whitewashed Parsonage, we were very glad to find that, although Mr. Chance had been gone for more than a week, Mrs. Chance and two of the children were still there; the furniture also had not been removed.

Mrs. Chance taught me to bake bread before she left, which was very useful, as I still often have to make camp bread. After a few days we were left alone with our boy Aleck. It was a primitive style of living, but we both enjoyed it immensely. The Indians were all so pleased to have us with them, and the attendance at services both on Sundays and Wednesday evenings was very satisfactory. There was something quite enchanting about our little log cottage, with the hops clambering up the verandah, the garden-beds full of flowers, the broad river in front of our windows, and the little sail-boat moored to the dock, which we could use at our will and pleasure. Then there were plenty of fish in the river, which the Indians brought to us, and an accommodating old duck laid an egg every morning just beside the door-step. Aleck was a capital boy; always cheery and ready, and would do anything he was asked to do. During our month's stay we only had fresh meat twice—once when a bear was killed, and again when we killed our drake. Among other duties of a new and peculiar kind, that of Post-master devolved upon me. The position was not an enviable one, and it took up a good deal of time; but it was convenient to get the mail without having to send twelve miles to Sault Ste. Marie for it. One day the boat arrived at the dock while we were at Church, and I had to set the people on singing a hymn while I ran down to change the mail. Another day an Indian came shouting at my window at 6 o'clock in the morning that the *Chicora* was just coming in. Half awake and half asleep I turned out of bed, seized the Post-office key, and in frantic haste rushed down to get my mail ready.

My wife sent Aleck running after me with my boots, which I had forgotten in my hurry! I was by this time able to preach to the Indians in their own tongue. On the first Sunday after our arrival we had an attendance of thirty-two persons at the Holy Communion, and among them were a good many young men. The offertory collection amounted to just £1 English money.

The first week in July we went on a little camping expedition to Echo River, where the Indians were making their birch-bark troughs ready for the next year's sugar-making. It was a fine bright morning when we started, and we went in *The Missionary*, with Aleck and two other Indian boys to row us. Echo River is a deep, narrow stream, scarcely a stone's throw wide, with the thick foliage of many and various trees overhanging its banks. The only sounds which broke the stillness were the notes of birds and the croaking of the bull-frog, mingled with the measured splash of the oars. At length, after about two hours' pull, we reached a little creek, and the Indian boys told us that their encampment was a short distance up it. It seemed scarcely possible to take the boat in, for the stream was very narrow, and nearly choked up with floating saw-logs. However, we pushed along with poles, and succeeded at length in reaching our destination. A good many of our people ran down and welcomed us heartily to their camp. It must have been strange to them, I suppose, to see a lady in so wild and out-of-the-way a spot.

A little clearing was cut with the axes, on which our tent was to be placed, and a path cut up to it from the creek; poles and tentpins were then made, and in a very short time our dwelling was ready for our reception. Meanwhile the fight with the lords of the Bush had commenced. While we were rowing we had not been much troubled with the mosquitoes, but now that we had invaded their dominions, they evidently regarded us as their lawful prey, and commenced the attack in good earnest. My wife, with a very serious face, drew on my large mackintosh coat, and sitting down on a heap of blankets, hid her hands, having first guarded her head and face with a thick veil. I filled the frying-pan with hot ashes, and covering them with green leaves, carried it in. The place was soon full of smoke, and after a vigorous whiffing I succeeded in making it habitable. Now we began to breathe a little more freely. Later in the afternoon we ventured on a short walk to see our neighbours. There were several wigwams all belonging to our own people. They were not conical, but had, generally, rounded roofs, over which were placed large sheets of birch-bark and Indian matting.

The people were very busy at work, the men drawing out saw-logs with two or three yoke of oxen; the women very busy with the birch-bark or basket-making. We found the Chief's wife sitting in a very airy apartment, there being nothing over her head but a few twisted sticks, on which the bark had not yet been laid. When we returned to our tent we found that good Aleck had already got the kettle boiling, and we made a capital supper off fried fish and potatoes. All was very comfortable. The Indians had put a thick layer of maple branches for a floor; on these were laid first a couple of Indian reed mats, and then our scarlet rugs and table cloth. After supper I sent Aleck to ask the Indians to come together for some singing. A great many collected, and we sang the "Te Deum" and several hymns in Ojebway. Then we sat round the camp fire, which blazed up cheerily and gave light enough for us to see our books. I was pleased to find how many of the people had their Ojebway prayer-books and testaments with them, carefully wrapped up in a pocket handkerchief. Each little knot of people lighted a small smouldering mosquito fire in the midst, so that smoke was rising on all sides. About ten o'clock I concluded with prayer; the people shook hands and departed. Rain was beginning to fall heavily. This and the clanging of cow-bells close outside the tent, and the music of mosquitoes trying to make their entrance through the net suspended over us, drove sleep from our eyelids. In the morning we had other enemies in the shape of minute sand-flies, smaller than a pin's head, which attacked us fiercely. It was no easy matter to light the fire in the morning in the drenching rain. One of the good people came up with an iron pot full of potatoes, which he hung over the fire to be cooked for our breakfast. When it ceased raining I went out to visit some of the people, and then we prepared to start homeward. We had only one Indian to help Aleck at the oars, and a head-wind to row against, so that it was late when we reached home; but, notwithstanding these drawbacks, we had enjoyed our trip.

The time for leaving Garden River was now drawing near, and the American steamer *St. Paul* was daily expected to pass. It would not stop at Garden River, but we should have to run out to it in our boat, so Aleck took up his position on the ridge of the roof to keep a look-out, and the first appearance of smoke round the point would be the signal for the boat to be got ready. I had frequently requested the stewards on the boats to bring me fresh meat from Collingwood on their up-trip.

They at length complied with my request, and just the day before we expected to leave came a big joint of thirteen pounds—the first we had seen since we came up. So we had beef for breakfast, beef for dinner, and beef for tea, and beef between times in the vain hope of getting through it. At last we called in our Indian friends and neighbours to partake, and they cleared off nearly all the food in the house. Evening came, and our boat had not arrived.

The next day was Sunday. Morning service was over, and the Indians, remembering the good feast of yesterday, came sniffing round, thinking to get another. We had a very spare luncheon, and we had to tell the Indians that we were quite out of victuals. Then we sent Aleck to the Jesuit priest to ask him if he would kindly send us a little butter and milk. In the evening the good man came down himself, and expressed the greatest distress at our laughable condition. He was a German by birth, but spoke English very well. "I think I have a leetle cock," he said, "and I will give him to you, and if you have some rice, you may make some soup; that will be better than to starve." We thanked him warmly, and Aleck went and brought the "leetle cock," and an Indian gave us a pint of huckleberries, and we scraped the flour-barrel and made a huckleberry pie, and so had quite a feast. On Monday morning the steamboat arrived, and we bade adieu to our Indian friends, and returned to Sarnia.

CHAPTER XIV.

Chief Little Pine.

Chief Little Pine (Augustin Shingwauk) was following his work in the lonely bush, his heart was sad at the thought of the black-coat (missionary) leaving them. Suddenly a thought entered his mind, it was as though an arrow had struck his breast; "I will go with him,—I will journey with this black-coat where he is going. I will see the great black-coat (the Bishop of Toronto) myself, and ask that Mr. Wilson may come and be our teacher, and I will ask him also to send more teachers to the shores of the great Ojebway Lake, for why indeed are my poor brethren left so long in ignorance and darkness with no one to instruct them? Is it that Christ loves us less than His white children? Or is it that the Church is sleeping? Perhaps I may arouse them, perhaps I may stir them up to send us more help, so that the Gospel may be preached to my poor pagan brethren. So I resolved to go. I only told just my wife and a few friends of my intention. I felt that the Great Spirit had called me to go, and even though I was poor and had but a few dollars in my pocket, still I knew that the great God in heaven, to whom forty years ago I yielded myself up, would not let me want. I felt sure that He would provide for my necessities. So when the raspberry moon had already risen, and was now fifteen days old (July 15), and the black-coat and his wife stepped on board the great fire-ship, I stepped on also. I had not told him as yet what was my object in going and at first he left me to myself, thinking, I suppose, that I was going on my own business. I was a stranger on board; no one knew me, and no one seemed to care for me.

"When we arrived at Ahmejewunoong (Sarnia), the fire-waggons (railway cars) were almost ready to start; so I still had to fast, and not until we had started on our way to Pahkatequayaug (London), did the black-coat know that I had been all that time without food. Then he was very sorry indeed, and from that time began to take great care of me, and I told him plainly what was my object in coming. It is not necessary for me to say anything about London. The black-coats met together in council to elect the great black-coat Chief (Bishop Hellmuth), and I went to the big church to see them all. But I had nothing particular to say to them, for their great black-coat had nothing to do with my people. I was impatient to get on to Toronto to see the chief black-coat who has authority to send teachers to my people on the great Ojebway Lake. We arrived in Toronto on the sixth day of the week when the raspberry moon was twenty-two days old. I was glad to see the great city again, for I had seen it first many years ago, when it was but a papoose, and had but a few houses and streets. We went to the place where the black-coats who have authority over missions meet, and I opened my heart to them and divulged its secrets. I said that at Garden River we were well content, for we had had the Gospel preached to us now for forty winters, and I felt our religious wants had been well attended to; but when I considered how great and how powerful is the English nation, how rapid their advance, and how great their success in every work to which they put their hands, I wondered often in my mind, and my people wondered too, why the Christian religion should have halted so long at Garden River, just at the entrance to the great Lake of the Ojebways; and how it was that forty winters had passed away and yet religion still slept, and the poor Indians of the great Ojebway Lake pleaded in vain for teachers to be sent to them. I said that we Indians know our great mother, the Queen of the English nation, is strong, and we cannot keep back her power any more than we can stop the rising sun. She is strong, her people are great and strong, but *my* people are weak. Why do you not help us? It is not good. I told the black-coats I hoped that before I died I should see a big teaching wigwam built at Garden River, where children from the great Ojebway Lake would be received, and clothed, and fed, and taught how to read and how to write, and also how to farm and build houses, and make clothing, so that by-and-bye they might go back and teach their own people. The black-coats listened to what I said, and they replied their wish was the same as mine. Afterwards I saw the Bishop of Toronto (Strachan), and he said that it was his own wish that Mr. Wilson should become our Missionary. My heart rejoiced more and more, and I felt now that the great object of my journey was accomplished, and I could return again to my people. But they did not wish me to go home yet. It was to be arranged that the white people should meet together to hear me speak on the third day of the following week.

"Many were the thoughts that filled my mind at that time, as I walked along the streets of Toronto, and looked at the fine buildings and stores full of wonderful and expensive things. 'How rich and powerful is the English nation!' I thought. 'Why is it that their religion does not go on and increase faster?' When I entered the place where the speaking paper (newspaper) is made, and saw the great machines by which it is done, and by which the papers are folded, I thought, 'Ah, that is how it is with the English nation, every day they get more wise, every day they find out something new. The Great Spirit blesses them and teaches them all these things because they are Christians, and follow the true religion. Would that my people were enlightened and blessed in the same way!'

"The next day was the day of prayer, and I went to the big wigwam where the children assemble to be taught. I stood up and spoke to them, and told them how much I desired that my children should be taught in the same way, and have such a beautiful wigwam to assemble in, where they might hear about God and His Son Jesus Christ. It rejoiced my heart to hear them sing. After this I entered the great house of prayer (the cathedral). I was in Toronto when the first one was there. Since that time it had been burnt down and rebuilt, and then all burnt down again, and yet now it stands here larger and grander than before. 'The white people,' I said to myself, 'have plenty of money; if they knew how poor my people are, surely they would give more of their money to build a house for us where our children may be taught.' I could not understand the words of the service, but my heart was full of thoughts of God, and I thought how good a thing it was to be a Christian, and I rejoiced that I had heard of the love of Christ, who died for His red children, as well as for the pale faces, for He is not ashamed, we know now, to call us brothers. During the few days we remained in Toronto I was out nearly all the time with Mr.

Wilson, collecting money at the people's wigwams. I am an old man of seventy winters, and I cannot walk about as much as I could when I was young; so he got a waggon, and we drove from house to house: I thought some of the people were very good. One woman gave us ten dollars, but many of them gave us very little, and some would not give us anything at all.

"When we reached St. Catharine's Mr. Wilson and myself went from wigwam to wigwam, asking for money to help the Indians on the great Chippeway Lake. In the evening the white people met together in the teaching wigwam, and there were so many of them that they had no more room to sit, and I spoke to them and told them the thoughts of my heart. This time I spoke more boldly than I had done before. I told them that as an Indian chief I had a right to speak on behalf of my poor people, for the land the white men now held was the land of my fathers; and now that the white man was powerful, and the Indian was weak, the Indian had a right to look to him for help and support. As I closed my speech I looked around last of all upon the children; for I wished my eyes last of all to rest upon these white children who had received the benefit of education and Christian instruction; and I gave them my beaver-skin to keep in their school, so that they might always remember my visit and think upon my words.

"On the second day of the week, early in the morning, we entered the fire-waggon to go to the river of the Mohawks. I was greatly rejoiced to see Mr. Chance once more, and also his wife and children. I remained with them three days.

"When the day came for me to leave, the black-coat, Chance, took me in his waggon to the place where the fire-waggons start, and sent a wire-message to Mr. Wilson to be ready to meet me when I arrived.

"I sat in the fire-waggon, and smoked my pipe, and rejoiced in my mind that my work was now over, and I should soon return to my people. For many hours I travelled, and the sun had already sunk in the west, and I thought I must be nearly arrived at Ahmujewunoong, when the fire-waggon chief came to look at my little paper; and then he looked at me and shook his head, and I understood I had come the wrong way. Presently the fire-waggon stood still, and the chief beckoned me to get out, and he pointed to the west, and made signs by which I understood that I must now wait for the fire-waggons going towards the sun-rising, and in them return part of the way back. By-and-bye the fire-waggons approached, coming from where the sun had set; and a man told me to get in. It was midnight when I reached Pahkatequayang (London), and they let me go into the wire-house and lie down to sleep. I slept well all night, and early in the morning a man beckoned to me that the fire-waggons were ready to start for Sarnia, and showed me which way to go.

"Thus I at length got back to Sarnia, and was glad to lie down and rest in Mr. Wilson's wigwam; and now I am waiting for the fire-ship to come, and as soon as it comes I shall go on board and return straight home to my people.

"The black-coat, Wilson. has asked me to let him write down all this that I have told him, so that it may be made into a book and read by everybody. And I hope that by-and-bye all the white people will see this book, and that their hearts will be warmed towards the poor ignorant Indians who live on the shores of the Great Ojebway Lake.

"We have collected three hundred dollars, but three hundred dollars is not enough to make religion increase. If we had but the worth of one of those big wigwams, of which I saw so many in Toronto, I think it would be enough to build a teaching wigwam at Garden River, and enough to send teachers also to the shores of the Great Ojebway Lake. I must have something done for my people before I die; and if I cannot get what I feel we ought to have from the Great Chiefs of this country, I am determined to go to the far distant land across the sea, and talk to the son of our Great Mother, the Prince of Wales, who became my friend during his visit to Canada, and gave me my medal, and who, I believe, will still befriend me if I tell him what my people need."

CHAPTER XV.

Our First Winter in Algoma.

SHORTLY after making this tour with Chief Little Pine, arrangements were made for our finally leaving Sarnia and removing our head-quarters to the Indian Mission at Garden River; the Committee of the Church Missionary Society agreed to the change as an experiment, and undertook to support the Mission for one year; but the withdrawal of the

New England Company and the fact of so many of the Indians having already been converted by the Roman Catholics, made them a little doubtful as to whether it would be a suitable spot for establishing one of their Missions permanently.

Before leaving Sarnia we had the satisfaction of seeing the little brick church on the Reserve completed and opened for use. This, together with the Kettle Point Mission, was now handed over to the charge of the native pastor, the Rev. John Jacobs.

I must mention one little incident that happened at this time. It was in the evening, and I had called to see Mr. Jacobs. He met me with his usual geniality, and we sat conversing for some time. Near the sofa was a large clothes-basket with a blanket over it. By-and-bye some little faint cries came from the neighbourhood of the basket. "What have you got there, Kesheg?" I asked. Mr. Jacobs was a little confused, and laughingly muttered something about an "arrival." The blanket was removed, and there lay two little mortals nestled together, one fair like his English mother, and the other dark like her father. The Indians afterwards gave them Indian names— "River Prince" and "River Princess."

It was the end of September when we left Sarnia. A little girl had been added to our family three weeks before. We had great difficulty in getting servants to go to so wild and out of the way a place as Sault Ste. Marie and Garden River were conceived to be. After many fruitless endeavours we were obliged to give it up, and took no one with us except our faithful Jane as nurse. There were no Canadian boats at that time running from Sarnia, so we had to take passage on an American vessel. We went well supplied with provisions sufficient to last us through the winter, and had all our furniture with us, besides horse, buggy, sleigh, and two cows. At that time there was but one clergyman in all the Algoma district, and he was located on the Manitoulin Island, 150 miles east of the point to which we were bound. To the west and north our nearest clerical neighbours would be the Missionaries of Hudson Bay and Rupert's Land, 500 or 600 miles away. It had been arranged that we should spend the winter at Sault Ste. Marie, a village of 300 or 400 people, twelve miles above the Garden River Mission, and a house had been engaged there for us to live in; the Church people at Sault Ste. Marie were anxious that we should do this,—a little stone church, St. Luke's, had just been built, and they, of course, were desirous to have regular services held; and I expected every Sunday to hold one service at Garden River, besides visiting the Indians during the week.

It was late on Saturday night, about 10 p.m., when we reached Sault Ste. Marie. The captain had kindly promised to put us off on the Canadian side, but it being so late and dark, and the channel not a safe one, he was unable to do so, and we were hurried off, boxes, tables, cows, horse, and all on the American dock. This placed us in a dilemma. Ten o'clock, Saturday night, and ourselves and our things all in the wrong place,—the right place being a mile and a-half across the water. The first thing to do under the circumstances was to take my family up to the hotel, after which I returned to the dock, and fortunately found a friend in need, Mr. Church, the owner of a sawmill on Sugar Island, a short distance below Garden River. He most obligingly undertook to put all my things across to the Canadian side for me. His men set to work with a will—several of them were Garden River Indians—and in a little time all was packed on board his scow, and we were steaming across the Ste. Marie River. Fortune, however, seemed to be against us,—we were about one-third of the way across when one of the cows who was tethered to a parlour stove jumped overboard, taking the stove along with her. Happily the rope broke, the stove sank, and the cow swam. A boat was put off, the cow taken in tow, and rowed back to the American side. However, in due time she was once more safely got on board and made fast, and in a little while we had reached our destination, and everything was landed at the Canadian dock. It was about one o'clock in the morning when I arrived there, and I went up to the empty Mission-house which we had occupied in the spring, and found a bed on which to snatch a few hours' rest.

On Sunday morning the Indians came round, all delighted, to see me again. After holding service in the church, I engaged two young Indians, and getting into *The Missionary*, we started for Sault Ste. Marie, as I was to have service there in the evening.

During the next day or two we were moving our furniture, &c. into this house which we had rented for the winter. It was roomy enough, but close to the river, and intolerably damp; so after a week or two of great discomfort we resolved on changing our quarters, and one fine morning, almost before light, saw *The Missionary* and another boat, loaded with our household effects, and running before a stiff breeze to Garden River. The Indians were delighted at the change, and all welcomed us warmly; but now fresh difficulties

THE OJEBWAY INDIANS.

arose: the little log parsonage was so cramped and small that we had nowhere to bestow our goods, and a considerable proportion of them had to be stowed away in the stable until two additional rooms could be built. It was rather late in the year for building operations, the winter being just about to commence; nevertheless we managed to secure the services of a couple of workmen, and in a little time a "balloon frame" was run up and two new rooms added to the house.

A terrible winter it was—one of the worst winters that had been known—the glass being sometimes from 30 to 40 below zero, and the snow very deep. One great snowdrift completely blocked the east end of the parsonage—it was about fifteen feet deep. The lower room was entirely dark, and we had to make a tunnel through the snow bank to let in the light. Some mornings it was so cold that we could not sit to the breakfast-table, but had all to huddle round the stove with our plates on our laps, and the empty cups that had been used when put back on the table froze to the saucers. Bread, butter, meat, everything, was frozen solid, and we began to realize what an Algoma winter was. But, apart from these discomforts, we had a very pleasant winter with our Indian friends; the services at the church were well attended, and there were generally upwards of thirty at the Holy Communion. At Christmas time we had a great feast; nearly a hundred of the people came, and after partaking of the good things, we gave them a magic lantern exhibition, which pleased them greatly. Then we always had service in the schoolhouse every Wednesday evening, at which there was an exceedingly good attendance; and on Friday evenings we held a cottage lecture, sometimes at one house, sometimes at another. Perhaps the most discouraging thing was the day-school. It is so hard to induce the Indians to send their children regularly to school. There may be thirty names on the register, but the average attendance is probably not more than nine or ten, possibly at times twelve to fifteen. It seems to be the same everywhere. The old people do not sufficiently realize the advantages of education themselves, and so seem to care little whether their children are in their place at class or roving about the bush with a bow and arrow. The Indians are great people for medicine. I had a good stock of it, and they were constantly coming to me with their ailments. They make medicines themselves from roots and herbs, but prefer generally to get the White man's physic. There was an old white-haired woman, an aunt of the chief's, who used to come stumping along with a thick stick, and caused some consternation in our nursery; she never knocked at the door—Indians rarely do—but would come in and sit herself down in the middle of the floor, the children scampering away to hide. She was a good-natured old creature, and of course would do no harm, but she frightened the children nevertheless.

We had one rather narrow escape while driving on the ice. It was on Christmas Day; I had been taking Morning Service at Sault Ste. Marie, and was driving back to Garden River with my wife and a young lady who was coming to stay with us; the wind was blowing, and the glass was in the neighbourhood of zero. All went well till we were within four miles of home; we had just passed a log cottage on the shore, and were striking out to cross a bay; we fancied we heard a shout behind us, but it was too cold to stop and look back; however it would have been better if we had done so, for a few moments more and our horse was plunging in the water, the rotten ice having given way beneath his feet. As quick as thought we all hurried out at the back of the sleigh and made for the solid ice. There were two or three inches of water on the ice, and our feet got wet, but otherwise we were safe from danger. In the meantime some Indians had seen us from the shore, and came running to us with a rope and some rails. It was twenty minutes before the poor horse was extricated; he was down in the water up to his neck, his eyes looked glassy, and I was afraid the poor thing was dying. However the Indians evidently knew what to do; they got the end of a rail under him as a lever to raise him up, and put a noose round his neck; then, having first loosened the harness, they pulled with a will, and in a few moments had him out of the hole kicking on the ice; they then gave him a good rubbing, and soon he made a plunge and was on his legs again, trembling and shaking; one of the young fellows took him off for a sharp trot to restore the circulation, then the sleigh was fixed up, and after a delay of about an hour we were enabled to continue our journey.

During the winter our mail was brought by men on snow-shoes with a dog train; they had to travel about 150 miles to a distant station, where they were met by other couriers, who exchanged bags with them and took them the remainder of the distance. The men go along at a jogging pace, and at night camp out in the snow.

CHAPTER XVI.

Chief Buhkwujjenene's Mission.

It was sugar-making time, and Buhkwujjenene was at work three miles back in the bush collecting the sap from the maple-trees, and, with the assistance of his wife and a large family of daughters, boiling it down in huge black kettles to transform it into maple-sugar. It was rather a labour getting out there, and I had to take my snow-shoes. About two miles back from where our parsonage stood is a long range of low, rocky hills, about 300 feet high, nearly parallel with the course of the river, and for the most part bare and naked, only sprinkled with a few ragged balsams, pine, and birch. It was April, and the snow was gone from the exposed parts of the hill, but beyond, in the valley where sugar-making was going on, it was still a couple of feet deep.

Wandering along through the bush, the first sign of your approach to a sugar-camp is generally the sound of an axe or the barking of a dog; these help to direct your steps; then, in a little while you see snow-shoe tracks, and then—here are the little birch-bark troughs, one or two to each maple-tree, and a slip of wood stuck in the tree about two feet from the ground, which serves as a spout to convey the sap from the tree to the trough. It does not run fast, about a drop in every three or four seconds, or sometimes much slower than that; however the little trough gets full in time, and then the Indians come round and pour it into birch-bark pails and carry it to the camp to be boiled. The sap is very nice when you are thirsty—slightly sweet and very cold, as the nights must be frosty during sugar-making time, and there is generally a little ice in each trough. Cold frosty nights and clear sun-shiny days is what the Indians like for their sugar-making. As soon as the weather gets too warm the sap becomes bitter and is no longer of any use.

Well, after my walk of course I took a draught of sap from the first trough I found, and then wended my way on to Buhkwujjenene's camp. The sugar camp is made of poles about four inches thick, laid horizontally for walls, and fitted into each other at the corners, the crevices being filled with moss. The walls are only about four feet high, and they enclose a space about ten or twelve feet square;

the roof is also made of poles placed like rafters and covered over with sheets of birch-bark, an opening being left the whole length of the ridge for the escape of the smoke. In the centre of the earthen floor is the fire, over which are suspended five or six large sugar-kettles, holding perhaps twenty or thirty gallons each, and into these the sap is poured as it is brought in from the trees. Along the inside of the wigwam on either side of the fire is a raised floor of boards or sticks, covered with fir branches, on which the Indians recline by day or sleep at night. The door is generally an old blanket hung over the opening. In just such a camp as this I found Chief Buhkwujjenene, for though chief of his band he yet has to hunt and fish and make sugar for his living, the same as the rest of his people.

" Ah-ah-ah boo-zhoo boo-zhoo!"—That's the way we Indians greet one another. Very warm and hearty, is it not? There they all were, busy over their big pots—Isabel and Susette and Therese and Liquette, and the old mother, who is very stout and comfortable-looking.

I told Buhkwujjenene that I wanted to have a little talk with him, so as soon as I had some maple syrup, and my pockets filled with sugar cakes to take home to the children, he came with me out of the wigwam, and we sat down on a log together for a pow-wow. Of course he lighted his pipe the first thing, for Indians can't talk without smoking. I told him I had been thinking that I would cross the great salt water to the land of the pale-faces, and try to collect some money to build the big teaching wigwam that we had been talking about, and I suggested the idea of taking him with me, if he would like to go. I said his brother "Little

Pine" had already done a good work by addressing meetings in Canada and thus giving a start to the scheme, and now it would be for him, the other chief, to carry the work on and help to raise funds sufficient to erect the institution. Buhkwujjenene listened attentively while I spoke, and then, laying his pipe down, replied as follows:

"It is true I have often thought that I would like to visit the great country across the great salt water, and I have sometimes thought that the day would come for me to do so; still, I am getting advanced in years now. I am no longer young as I used to be. I am not always well, and it is a long way to go. Nevertheless I am willing to accompany you if the Great Spirit wills it. I committed myself to the hands of the Great Spirit when I became a Christian forty years ago. If it is His will that I should go, I will go; if it is not His will I will stay here."

A few days after this the Indians held a council in the school-house, when it was definitely arranged that Buhkwujjenene should accompany me to England, and the Indians agreed to sell an ox, which belonged to them in common, to assist in defraying his expenses.

The party who were to make the trip across the Atlantic consisted of Mrs. Wilson, our little boy Archie (whom the Indians call Tecumseh, after the celebrated chief who fought under Sir Isaac Brock in 1812), Chief Buhkwujjenene, and myself. We started on a bright Monday morning towards the middle of May, the first part of our journey being accomplished in the steam-boat *Waubuno*, which took us as far as Collingwood, a distance of 300 miles. From Collingwood we took train about 100 miles to Toronto, where we staid a few days;

then from Toronto we took train *via* Niagara and Buffalo to New York. Our train arrived a few hours only before the steamship *The India* was to start.

So far Chief Buhkwujjenene had seen nothing more than he had seen before in his life, for he had already on more than one occasion travelled through Canada. Now however that he was embarked on an ocean steamer, all would, for the next few months, be new to him. One of his first experiences was the qualms of sea-sickness, and I verily believe he thought he was going to die. However, as with the white man so with the Indian, a few days on the salt water set him all right, and strength, spirits and appetite returned. One evening on deck he told me a dream he had had shortly before I proposed for him to accompany me. "I thought I was working outside my house," he said, "when I heard the note of a loon. (The loon is a favourite bird among the Indians, and they regard it with superstitious reverence.) The sound came from the Western sky, and I gazed in that direction to try if I could see the bird. In another moment I heard the sweep of its wings over my head, and there it flew sailing majestically along and drawing after it an airy phantom ship with three masts; it sailed away off east, still uttering its monotonous note till it was lost to view. Thus my dream has come true," he said, "for this is the three-masted vessel that I saw in my dream, and the loon is dragging us along!"

At length the north coast of Ireland came in sight, and then the Scotch coast, and finally we came to anchor in the harbour at Greenock. It was late in the evening, about 8 p.m., when we arrived, and we heard that there was a through train to London at 8.30, so we made a great effort to catch it; we succeeded in boarding the train at the very last moment, and were off by the night mail to London.

The next morning there appeared the following interesting, though not very truthful, notice in the

Glasgow Herald:—" An interesting stranger has arrived in this country, and it may possibly turn out that the 'Coming Man' has come at last. His name, we understand, is Chief Buhkwujjenene, which signifies 'a man of the Desert,' and he landed in Greenock from the Anchor Line steamer *India*. The man was dressed in the full costume of the

Chippewa tribe, to which he belongs, namely, skins, feathers, &c. He is described as being tall and handsome, with a frank but thoughtful face, and appeared to be about thirty years of age. It is understood that this chief, who proceeded immediately per mail train to London, has been converted to Christianity, and has been brought over to England under the auspices of the Church of England Missionary Society, in order that he may be instructed in Christian truth, fitting him to return as a native teacher and preacher among his tribe in the backwoods of America. A more appropriate lodging for 'a man of the Desert' cannot be found in the whole world than Leicester Square; though whether he would receive much Christian truth in that locality is another question. If he would send for his tribe, and encamp there permanently, a picturesque effect might be produced at a very trifling outlay."

We travelled all night, and were due at Euston Square the following day. Early the next morning we sent on the following telegram to announce our arrival to our unexpecting friends:—"Myself, wife, Archie, and Indian chief have arrived; shall reach Euston at 3 p.m." This was the first intimation that our friends had of the certainty of our paying them a visit, as we had come away by the first boat down on the opening of navigation, and our letters sent by dog-sleigh a week or two before that were still on the road. Still less had they any expectation of an introduction to one of the natives of our wild backwoods.

Our train steamed into Euston Square punctual to the time after its long run of 400 miles. And now familiar sights met our eyes after a four years' absence from our native land; there were the cabs and the running porters and the dense crowd of people filling the station; and there—still more familiar sight—was my father's carriage and the well-known figure of our coachman on the box. Then came hearty shakes of the hand from my father and brother who had come to meet us, and Chief Buhkwujjenene, who seemed quite lost, poor man, among the excitement and bustle, was introduced and shook hands with the venerable English Black-coat.

It was strange the affection that Buhkwujjenene conceived for my brother from the first; he misunderstood his name (Arthur), and thinking it to be Otter, always called him *Neegig*. Upon my father he conferred the name of *Pashegonabe*, the great eagle, and one of my sisters he was pleased to call *Wabausenooqua*, which title he explained to mean a little spot cleared by the wind; though for what reason he gave this name we could never quite make out. *Neegig* and he became great friends; they had one thing in common, and that was a love for tobacco, and in the summer evenings after dinner the young white man and his grown companion would recline on rustic seats in the garden, and smoke pipe after pipe, the red man mixing his " baccy" with some savoury bark from his native land which he produced from the depths of his martin-skin tobacco-pouch. They could not understand each other's speech, but by dint of signs and a few broken words of English occasionally introduced by the Chief, they managed to carry on some conversation.

Quite a sensation was caused not only in the house but in the neighbourhood by the new-comer's arrival. It was strange to see him sitting in his blanket coat in an easy chair beneath the gaslights in the drawing-room, strange to see him conducting a lady in to dinner and sitting at table awaiting the arrival and removal of the various courses, strange to see him walking the streets with his medals on his breast, his skunk skin and leggings and feather in his hat, or riding in the same attire on the top of an omnibus; and yet amid it all he bore himself with such perfect grace and self-possession that every one admired and wondered at him. People thought he had a very pleasant expression and agreeable manner, and they were astonished at his politeness and the cool self-possessed way in which he accepted the many new experiences which kept crowding upon him. A photographer in the neighbourhood soon heard of his arrival and asked him to sit for his portrait. Several likenesses were taken—representing him as a Christian Chief in his ordinary dress; and as a Chief of former days in feathers and Indian costume. As he could scarcely speak a word of English I was obliged to be tied rather closely to him as interpreter, and assist him in receiving visitors, numbers of whom came almost daily. We also had a visiting-card prepared for him on which was inscribed Chief Buhkwujjenene, Garden River, Canada. At morning and evening prayers and in church on Sundays he was most devotional, and whenever the Lord's prayer was repeated he joined audibly in the Indian tongue—" *Wayoosemegooyun keezhegoong ayahyun, tah keche-ahpeetandahgwud kedezhenekausoowin,*" &c.

CHAPTER XVII.

An Indian Chief in England.

WE were not long in setting the Chief to work. It was Friday when we arrived, and on the following Thursday our first meeting was held in Bishop Wilson's Memorial Hall, Islington. Notice was given of the meeting in church on the intervening Sunday, the Chief occupying a seat in one of the pews, and a circular was also issued headed:—

"A RED INDIAN CHIEF'S VISIT TO ENGLAND."

The result was an overflowing meeting. The vicar occupied the chair and a number of clergy were on the platform. Chief Buhkwujjenene seeming to be just as much at his ease as if he were addressing a council of his own people, stood forth and in simple eloquent terms told his story, myself interpreting for him every time he paused.

"My brothers and sisters, he began, I salute you. I have come all the way across the great salt water to see you, and it does my heart good to see so many pale faces gathered together before me." He then recounted what had led him to take the journey. It had not been his own wish, but he felt that God had led him to do so; God had preserved him amid the dangers of the ocean, and he trusted that God would prosper the cause for which he came to plead. Many years ago, he said, I and my people were in a very different state to what we are now: we had no teaching, no churches, no missionaries, our medicine men taught us to believe in good and bad spirits and to depend on dreams. I, when a boy, was obliged by my father to blacken my face and fast for many days together, and while doing this it was believed that whatever I dreamed would come true. But now we Indians at Garden River are no longer heathen, we have all now accepted Christianity and we have our church and our missionary. The desire of my heart is to see our religion spread among the other Indians; we want more Missionaries to be sent

to us, and greater efforts made to extend the blessings of the Gospel. We want our children to be taught to follow civilized trades as the white people do. We feel that the time is past for the Indians to live by hunting and fishing as our forefathers used to do. We wish to give up our old habits and adopt the customs of the pale faces. In order to accomplish this we propose that a big teaching wigwam should be built at Garden River where our sons may be taught to carpenter and make boots and other such things as are useful, and where our daughters may learn needlework and knitting and spinning. This is the desire of my heart, this is the cause for which I have come to plead. We Indians are too poor to help ourselves, and so we look to you white people who now occupy our hunting grounds to help us. We know that our great Mother Queen Victoria, loves her Indian subjects; often have we fought for her and we are ready to fight her battles again. We have readily given up our hunting grounds to you, and all that we ask of you is that you will help us in improving ourselves and in educating our children."

After this the Chief put on his Indian dress and sang a war song. Much interest was stirred up by his address and the collection which was made after the meeting amounted to upwards of £11.

The following Sunday the Holy Communion was administered at the old parish church of St. Mary's, and among those who knelt at the rails to receive the sacred emblems of our Lord's passion and death, was the Indian Chief Buhkwujjenene. I repeated the words to him in his own tongue as I administered the bread and wine.

The following day we visited the Rev. Henry Venn, the venerable Secretary of the Church Missionary Society. He received us most kindly, and for his own part he hoped that the Committee, whom we were to meet on the morrow, would agree to continue their support of the mission at Garden River, and to assist us in our proposed scheme for the advancement and civilization of the Indians; he feared, however, we might have some difficulty in the matter, on account of our proposed plans not being strictly in accordance with the main object of the Society, which is to carry the Gospel to the heathen.

Among the earliest plans made for the edification and amusement of the Chief was a visit to the Zoological Gardens at Regent's Park. Among the birds the Chief quickly recognized the Canadian thrush, and doffed his hat with evident pleasure at the rencontre. We went the regular rounds, as every one does, through the monkey-house, through the parrot-house, down through the tunnel and alongside the canal to the house of the reptiles, then back to where the elephants and giraffes are kept. The hippopotamus was on land so we saw him well; the giraffes walked round and round and bowed their necks to the visitors as they always do ; the elephant obeyed his keeper, stood up on his hind legs, elevated his trunk, trumpeted and consumed biscuits. Then we saw the lions and tigers fed. The Chief had a ride on one of the camels, and looked very picturesque in his white blanket coat, though scarcely oriental enough in his appearance to produce a natural effect.

Another day we had an interview with his Royal Highness the Prince of Wales. It was not brought about in the way such things are generally accomplished, but still it did very well. The occasion was the opening of the Bethnal Green Museum. We had gallery tickets for the Chief and myself. It was an imposing display. The centre of the hall was occupied by all the great grandees in brilliant dress, including natives of many a foreign clime. The arrival of Royalty was signalized by a clarion blast which thrilled through one's veins and set one on the tiptoe of expectation. The Royal party entered, the necessary ceremonies for the opening of the building were gone through, and then commenced .

THE OJEBWAY INDIANS. 105

a tour of the galleries. The Prince and his suite would pass close to us. This was a chance not to be thrown away. I had a photograph of Buhkwujjenene in my pocket. Buhkwujjenene on his breast wore a silver medal presented to him in common with other chiefs by the Prince on the occasion of his visit to Canada some years before. I stepped up to one of the managers of the Institution—Here was an Indian chief, a medal on his breast, given him by the Prince of Wales. Would it be out of place for the Chief to present his *carte de visite* to the Prince? The manager good-naturedly said that he would speak to one of the suite when they approached and ask if it could be done. Soon the word came that the Prince would be pleased to have Chief Buhkwujjenene presented to him. So space was made for us by a policeman in the front ranks of the crowd—and we awaited His Royal Highness's arrival. The moment came. His Royal Highness greeted the Chief most cordially and pleasantly, examined the medal on his breast, and said that he remembered his face among the Indian chiefs who had been presented to him in Canada. "Tell him," said the Prince to me; "tell him I remember his face perfectly." We were then permitted to join the Royal procession and make the round of the building.

But our time was not all taken up in sight-seeing. We had plenty to do, and only a little time to do it in. Nearly every night there was a meeting, and often we had two or three engagements in the course of a day. Never did an Indian chief have such a hard time of it. Wherever he went, he wore his blanket coat, his feather in his hat, his leggings and moccasins, and the skunk skin on his arm. Very seldom was any attempt made to treat him rudely, though occasionally it was necessary to hurry him through the streets to avoid a crowd collecting. Wide guesses were made at his nationality; one would take him for a New Zealander, another for a native of Japan.

One of our best meetings was a garden-party at

Mitcham Vicarage. There was a large gathering of ladies and gentlemen beneath the dark spreading cedars on the soft lawn. The Chief put on his feathers and ornaments, and at once became the centre of attraction. I think it was on this occasion that he narrated the Indian tradition of the Flood.

"Nanaboozhoo," said the Chief, "had a son. He loved his son. He told his son never to go near the water lest evil should come to him. The son disobeyed his father: he went out in a canoe and was never seen or heard of more. Nanaboozhoo then vowed vengeance against the gods of the water, who had destroyed his son. There were two of these gods, and one day they lay sleeping on the shore. Nanaboozhoo was looking everywhere for them, determined to kill them. A loon offered to show him where they were sleeping. He followed the loon till he found them, and then he made short work of them with his tomahawk and his war-club. But lo, and behold, no sooner were the gods dead than the waters of the great lake rose up in vengeance; they pursued Nanaboozhoo up on to the dry land, and he had to run for his life. He sought the highest mountain and climbed to the top of the highest pine-tree. Still the waters pursued him. They rose higher and higher. What could he do? He broke off a few of the topmost branches, and made a raft upon which he got and saved himself. He saved also a number of the animals that were kicking and struggling in the water all around him. At length he bethought himself of making a new world. How should he do it? Could he but procure a little of the old world he might manage it. He selected the beaver from among the animals, and sent it to dive after some earth. When it came up it was dead. He sent the otter, but it died also. At length he tried the musk rat. The musk rat dived. When it came up it was dead. But in its claws was clenched a little earth. Nanaboozhoo carefully took this earth, rubbed it in his fingers till it was dry, then placed it in the palm of his hand, and blew it gently over the surface of the water. A new world was thus formed, and Nanaboozhoo and all the animals landed. Nanaboozhoo sent out a wolf to see how big the world was. He was gone a month. Again he sent him out, and he was gone a year. Then he sent out a very young wolf. This young wolf died of old age before it could get back. So Nanaboozhoo said the world was big enough, and might stop growing."

About £80 was collected on this occasion.

We paid two visits to the Archbishop of Canterbury, at Lambeth. On both occasions he was most cordial and kind, and appeared to take much interest in the work of evangelizing the Indians.

CHAPTER XVIII.

A Trial of Faith.

AFTER this, meetings were held at Hastings, Reading, Eynsford, Bayswater, Hampstead, Tooting, Wimbledon, Coleshill, Kensington, Ware, and many other places; all much of the same character —money was collected, and photographs and articles of birchbark sold. The Chief excited much interest by recounting the circumstances of his own conversion to Christianity. "When I was a little boy, not older than that little fellow there," he said, pointing to a child in the assembly, "I was very badly off. My mother was dead, and my father loved the fire-water. I was often cold and hungry, and at night would sometimes crawl into the wigwam and lie down beside my drunken father. After I was grown older, a preacher came into our neighbourhood and began to preach the Gospel to the Indians, and I used to go sometimes to listen to him. I thought the words he spoke were very wonderful, and I was so much impressed by them that I took every opportunity I could of going to listen. As for my father, he would not go to hear the preaching, and he did not wish me to go, but I used to go secretly without telling him. One evening I was going as usual to hear the Missionary speak, wending my way alone through the dark lonely bush. My path led me out into a clearing where I could see the distant horizon, and the sun was setting in great splendour, the heavens all lighted up with gold and crimson. Suddenly, like an arrow, there darted into my breast the words which I had heard the preacher use about the last great day when the Saviour would return again in glory surrounded by all the holy angels. I sank upon my knees, and there and then offered up my first prayer to God. The next morning I called on the Missionary, and told him that I wished to become a Christian, and a short time after that I was baptized. Some time after this I was very sick, and my life was despaired of. My father, though disapproving of my having accepted Christianity, was nevertheless very fond of me; he was much grieved that I was sick, and I noticed that he had begun to think more seriously of the Christian religion, for I had often spoken to him and urged him to become a Christian; I had also prayed constantly to God that He would change my father's heart. One day my father came to me as I still lay sick upon my bed, and he said to me, 'My son,

Buhkwujjenene, I do not know whether you will get well again or not, for I know you are very sick indeed, but I wish to tell you this, that I have resolved to become a Christian, and to-morrow morning myself and all your brothers and sisters are going to the Missionary to be baptized.'"

It was a sore blow to us when word came from the Secretary of the Church Missionary Society that the Committee had decided not to continue the Garden River Mission.

It was to me a great trial of faith to be told that my choice lay between accepting a more lucrative post in Rupert's Land or relinquishing connection with the Society under whose auspices I had first gone forth. What was I to do? How could I break the distressing news to my poor friend Buhkwujjenene? I went down upon my knees, and laid the matter before my God in prayer. And very soon the answer came. A letter was put into my hand which said, "A friend will guarantee you £100 a year if you will remain at your post at Garden River." How I thanked God. I felt it was His hand directing, and I at once accepted the offer. The Colonial and Continental Church Society guaranteed a yearly grant, and I was sure that we were being led by God, and that all would be right. I could meet my poor Chief now with a bright face and a light heart. I could tell him that all was well; that the Garden River Mission would be permanently established, and that the "big teaching wigwam" should (D.V.) be built.

The next thing was to organize an English Committee and to open a subscription list for the support of the proposed Institution. Among them were the late Ven. Archdeacon Hunter, of Bayswater, and the Rev. J. Halcombe.

A circular which was issued stated that the Chief had been greatly encouraged by the sum of money (£740) already collected towards the object he had so much at heart, and that the object of the Committee was to further the good Chief's wishes by the erection of an Industrial School at Garden River, where children both of Christian and of pagan parents from all parts of the Ojebway territory, would be received, clothed, boarded, educated, instructed in Christian truth, and also taught to farm and to follow useful employments. The Committee did not expect to do anything great at once, but to begin with small things, and gradually extend their work as the way might open. The amount required for the annual support of the Mission would be at least £600. It was expected that the Canadian Government would make a grant towards the support of the Institution when once fairly started, and the hope was expressed that many friends would be found both in England and in Canada to assist, so that the poor Indians might not be left destitute and uncared for, but rather learn that it was the wish of their white friends, while sending them the good tidings of salvation, also to help them to become prosperous and happy in this life, and enable them to maintain their rights as original owners of the soil.

These steps having been thus satisfactorily taken and money sufficient collected to make a commencement, it seemed unnecessary to keep the good Chief away any longer from his home, and one day in the first week in August we put him on board a steamboat in London Docks and started him off for Quebec. He preferred thus to go alone rather than wait to accompany our party a month later, as he wanted to get home to see to his cattle and crops and make provision for the winter. I gave him a letter, with full directions as to time of trains, &c., which he could show to any one, and Indians are always clever in finding their way about, so that I felt no anxiety about him. When I met him afterwards at Garden River, he pointed to his little log cottage, and said that was better than all the great houses in England. However, he retained very pleasing recollections of his visit, and often has he since asked me to write a letter for him to one or another of the good friends whom he made while in the country of the pale faces.

When we started on our homeward voyage, about a month later, we took with us a young man from the Rev. D. B. Hankins' congregation at Ware, named Frost, to be school teacher at the Institution when built, and also a man and his wife from a farm in Kent as servants. On board the steamboat we fell in with a family of emigrants, and persuaded them to accompany us to Sault Ste. Marie. The man was a carpenter by trade, and helped us in many ways, but the following year he fell ill and died. We then took the widow into our employment as laundress, and she is with us still. Our two younger children who had been with their nurse at London, Ontario, during our absence, now rejoined us, and we were soon once more settled and ready for a second Algoma winter.

CHAPTER XIX.

LEARNING TO KNOW MY PEOPLE.

The Indians are a people requiring a good deal of patience on the part of their teachers, as those who have tried working among them have generally found. There is on the one hand a charming fascination about their simple manners and habits, their readiness to receive and accept Gospel teaching, the bright winning smile that lights up their faces when pleased, their stoical behaviour under adverse circumstances, their gentleness and politeness, the absence of that rough manner and loud talk which is so common among white people of the lower classes; and yet on the other hand we must admit that there are certain strong points in their natural character which are anything but pleasing; and it is, I believe, these points coming to the notice of people who are not inclined to befriend them that have earned for them the character of an idle, ungrateful people. Many a time has it been said to me, "How can you waste your time working among those Indians? They will never get any better for all you can teach them or do for them." And yet I have continued labouring, and do still labour among them, believing that it is God's will that every wandering sheep should be sought out and, if possible, be brought into the Good Shepherd's fold. If at times I have found them trying, yet, after all, I doubt if they are much more so than many a community of white people.

I will now give a few extracts from my journal of the winter 1872-73.

Oct. 21, we were up at 5.30 a.m., preparing for the "Bee;" I rang the church bell to bring the Indians together, and hoisted the Union Jack. Mrs. Cryer got tea made, and pork and potatoes cooked, and about 7.30 a.m. twelve stalwart Indians sat down to breakfast. Then axes were shouldered, the oxen yoked, and we started for the farm land a little way back from the house. We mustered

twenty-two in all and had a good days' work— chopping down trees and brush-wood, grubbing up roots, and making huge fires to burn all up. About twelve acres were cleared sufficiently for ploughing, and this will be fenced round. In the evening, when the men all came in for supper, I showed then my plans for the new buildings, and they seemed very much pleased with them. Later in the evening I was asked to come in to Buhk-wujjenene's house, as they wished to settle the matter about the ox.

Nov. 21.—The Indians held a great council in the school-house this evening. Chief Buhkwujjenene was the principal speaker. He spoke very eloquently, feelingly, and quite to the point,—describing his journey to England and his kind reception by so many friends there. Then he spoke of the proposed Institution, for which money had been collected, and told the people that an opportunity was now given them of improving themselves and their children, and he urged upon all to support the movement and to give up their children to be educated. Chief Little Pine spoke of the increasing value of their land and the desire of the white people to purchase it from them. Our wealth, he said, is our land. As long as it lies idle it is worthless. We must clear our land and farm it, and then it will be of the greatest value. He also spoke of the Institution, and advised the people to send their children. Misquaubuhnooke and Shabahgeezhik also spoke, and each found fault with the Indians for not exerting themselves more; they said the congregations were not large enough on Sundays, and that many of the people who had families did not send their children to school.

Dec. 1, *Advent Sunday.*—Heavy snow falling, but good congregations. I preached from Rom. xiii. 12. "The night is far spent, the day is at hand; let us therefore cast off the works of darkness, and let us put on the armour of light." We have commenced a weekly offertory, and it amounts to nearly two dollars a Sunday. Two churchwardens have been appointed, and one of them has charge of the Church funds and is supposed to purchase all that is necessary in the way of fuel, oil, &c. The collections ought to be ample to meet all expenses besides paying the sexton; but if not constantly watched the Indians are apt to spend the money on things not really wanted, while we are shivering for want of fire, and blinding ourselves for want of light.

Dec. 27.—Evening Communicants' meeting at William Shabahgeezhik's; about twenty-five present. I spoke very plainly to the people, and urged none to come forward to the Sacrament without due preparation. I said I would rather see ten persons kneeling at the rail and feel that they were truly in earnest, than thirty people who had come forward without thinking of what they were doing. I invited them to come and talk with me individually in private. I said God had brought me to this place to be their friend and counsellor, and to help them on their road to heaven, and I hoped that they would regard me as such.

Dec. 28.—Our first winter mail arrived to-day. The first mail we hear was lost and one of the couriers drowned, so this must be the second that has now arrived. I had only just brought up a large packet of letters and papers to the house, when I was called away three miles distant, to see a man who had been taken suddenly ill and was supposed to be dying. I went in the sleigh and administered medicine to him. Then came a call in an opposite direction to see Chief Little Pine, who is also sick. He has no serious symptoms, but is very weak, and eats nothing. He says he does not wish to say anything about his illness, and wants no medicine. "The great God," he said, "knows all, and He can take care of me."

Dec. 29, *Sunday.*—We had twenty-seven at Holy

Communion to-day,—little over half the number that assembled last year. I take this for a good sign. I trust that our people are beginning to think more, and to realize how solemn is this Holy Feast. The offertory collection was nearly four dollars. This I take for the relief of the sick. On the other Sundays the money is used for church expenses.

Jan. 3, 1873.—Meeting to-night at Peter Jones'— about twenty-four present. After it was over I told the people that the meeting next week would be at Misquaubuhnooke's, on Sugar Island, and we had made a plan for Mr. Frost to go over and teach school there three times a week. I also made some reference to the dancing, in which they so much indulge at this time of the year,—exhorting them not to keep up their parties late at night, to finish with reading and prayer, and not to be ashamed for the Bible to be seen on the table; also not to let the whiskey bottle appear. I said God willed that we should enjoy ourselves, but in our enjoyment we must remember Him, and not give way to sin.

Jan. 4.—Yesterday, while out, I was called in to see a poor boy in a very suffering state, a large piece of cord-wood having fallen on his arm and created some internal injury. The accident happened five days ago, and nothing yet had been done. I immediately applied a cooling lotion. The poor little fellow, who is only about thirteen years old, was in great pain. His home is some three miles off, on Sugar Island, and his mother had only heard of the accident to-day, and had just arrived when I was called in. This morning I have brought him up in the sleigh to my house and placed him on a bed in the little old school-house; there is a nice fire in the stove, and we have given the mother cooking utensils and food, so they will be quite comfortable.

Jan. 5.—About eleven o'clock last night the poor boy's mother came knocking for me at the window; so I went over to see him. He seemed much worse, and was screaming with the pain; his arm was quite black and the inflammation extending to the hand. The mother seemed in great trouble, and, being Roman Catholics, I told her I would go over to see the priest, and perhaps he would send some one to the Sault for the doctor. The priest came back with me, but seemed to think it no use to send for the doctor, as, if mortification was beginning, he could do no good. I then left the priest alone with him, while I went to prepare a soothing draught. While walking with the priest, I took the opportunity to say a few words to him about my visiting his people. I told him I was often called in by his people to visit their sick ones, and hitherto had made it rather a point of honour not to speak to them about religion, as I thought he would not like it, and only on one occasion had done so. I, however, did not like this plan; as a clergyman I felt that I ought to have the privilege of speaking to those whom I was called on to visit, especially the dying; so, if he objected to my doing so, it would be best for him to tell his people not to send for me. The priest said he certainly should not like his people to be talked to; still he would be sorry for me to give up visiting the sick, and "if I wished sometimes to offer words of consolation I must do so."

At the close of my sermon to-day I mentioned this circumstance to our people, showing them first of all the difference between our religion and that of the Roman Catholics—the latter shut the Bible up, we give it to all; the latter teach people to depend on the priest for everything. we point only to God and to Jesus Christ. I said I indeed desired to see all the people on this Reserve members of our Church; still I felt that this would not be effected by strife and quarrelling, but only by love. I wished, I said, to try and copy the Saviour, who loved all men alike. For this reason, when called to help Roman Catholics or to give them medicine, I was willing to do so, as I thought it was right to do so. Still I had long felt dissatisfied that my tongue should be tied when visiting these people, for fear of offending the priest. For that reason I had now had a talk with the priest, and told him that in future, if I visited his people, I must be allowed to talk to them. If he did not like me to do this, he must forbid them sending for me. A good many of our people went in after service to see the poor sick boy. I took Archie in also to see him. The boy seemed much pleased to see him, saying, 'Kagat minwahbumenahgooze' (he is very pretty), and afterwards repeated the same words to his mother when she came in.

Jan. 7.—This evening I had quite a nice talk with my poor boy-patient. I told him the story of God's love in sending His Son to die for us; also about the penitent thief on the cross being saved in his last hour of life. The child listened very attentively, and appeared to drink in all that I told him, and I then knelt by his bed-side and prayed for him.

Jan. 10.—My poor boy is, I hope, getting a little better. His arm gives him less pain. I again had a little talk with him, and prayer. I asked him if he thought God treated him hardly in sending him so much suffering, and he replied, "No." I then told him that God had certainly sent it all in love for his soul, so that he might be led to think and prepare for the future life: God had already heard our prayers for him, and if he should get quite well, I hoped he would always love and serve God.

Jan. 19.—Frost has begun his school on Sugar Island. The first day he had thirteen children and the second day fourteen. He is getting on wonderfully with the Indian language, and can read the lessons in church.

Feb. 2, *Sunday.*—To-day we had about seventy at morning service, and twenty-seven communicants. Chief Little Pine came yesterday to see me about the Holy Communion. He said that recently I had spoken so strongly about the danger of receiving it unworthily that he was afraid. I knew, he said, that he owed Penny over twenty dollars; also that he had not yet paid his promised subscription of ten dollars to the school. I told him God knew the secrets of all our hearts. If he really intended to pay what he was owing as soon as possible, it was not sin for him to be in debt, and he might partake of the Sacrament with a clear conscience. I was rather glad, however, to see him turn away at the end of the service. It is the first time that he has done so, and I trust he is really beginning to think more of what it all means.

CHAPTER XX.

A Wedding and a Death.

Feb. 3, 1873.—To-day William Buhkwujjenene, the Chief's only son, was married to Philemon Atoosa. The wedding was appointed for 10 a.m., and early in the morning William was off to fetch his bride and her party, their house being about four miles off, on Sugar Island. It was long past the hour when Buhkwujjenene, Atoosa, and several other Indians came to me in a rather excited state, and Buhkwujjenene, as spokesman, explained that, although Atoosa, the father, was willing for his daughter to be married in our church, the mother and brother were opposed, and wanted the priest to marry them. I replied briefly that there were two religions, Roman Catholic and Church of England. When marriages took place between parties of different Churches, agreement must be made in which Church they would be married; this agreement had already been made in this case, banns had been published, and the bride and her father were both willing, so there was no need for any trouble. Chief Buhkwujjenene said that was enough, and he would go for the party. However, I waited on and on, and at length went over to Buhkwujjenene's house to ascertain the cause of delay. I found that he, Atoosa, and his son, had gone over to see the priest. They soon returned, and brought word that the priest raised no objection to the marriage being performed in our Church, and had even said, " If you do what is right in the

Church of England you will go to heaven the same as if you belonged to the Roman Catholic Church;" rather liberal language for a Jesuit priest.

It was now past noon, and still there came one cause of delay after another, so that it was 1.45 p.m. before the party had actually assembled in the church. All passed off very well. Bride and bridegroom put their marks in the register, and then all repaired to Chief Buhkwujjenene's dwelling. The bride wore a blue merino dress with green trimmings, a smart crimson necktie, gold brooch, chain, and locket, her hair in a net with blue ribbons. The bridesmaids were Isabel, Nancy, Sophy, and Therese Weesaw.

The feasting began at 2.30 p.m., the table very well spread—wedding-cake, wine, turkey, goose, rabbit, beef, tarts, buns, and preserves! About twenty-five sat down at a time, the bride and bridegroom at the head. Two tables were cleared before the speeches began. Chief Little Pine made a capital speech, relating the happiness of his own married days, and wishing for a like blessing on the young couple just united.

March 15.—Last evening our cottage reading was at Buhkwujjenene's. I had just given out the first hymn when a message came that I was wanted immediately at George Pine's, for Eliza was very ill, and, they feared, dying. I got my medicines and jumped into the sleigh. George Pine had gone away last Monday beaver-hunting. Only Sarah was in the house. Eliza was lying on a couch on the floor, her head to the wall, her feet toward the stove,—Sarah sitting about two yards from her on the floor by the wall, with Eliza's baby on her knees. The other two little children, Benjamin and Esther, were lying on some blankets on the floor at the other side of the room. While I was taking off my cap and muffler George Angisteh bent down and looked at Eliza, and then said to Sarah, "She is dead!" He then got up quickly, and went out to summon the neighbours. In the meantime I felt her pulse and heart, but her eyes were fixed, and she evidently was dead; the women who came in tried rubbing her arms and legs, but without any effect. Gradually the room became crowded with persons, the two chiefs among the number. I gave a short address, expressed my belief that Eliza was fully prepared for death, and was now happy; and told the people her words about the eight true Christians whom she thought might be found in Garden River. I pitied, I said, the three little orphan children, and I trusted that God would care for them. I spoke to Benjamin, the eldest (six years old), and told him his mother was in heaven, and that he must try and love God, and then he would go to see her again by-and-bye.

March 18.—To-day was the funeral. The church was crammed. I gave a short address after the lesson, and we sang a hymn. The coffin was opened in the church that all who wished might take a last look. This is a prevalent custom with the Indians. There was no road cut to the cemetery, so I had to go on snow-shoes, and the sleigh, with the coffin, was drawn by four men. Again at the grave I said a few words, and commended the three little orphan children to God's care.

May 28.—A very satisfactory meeting to-night. After the usual evening service was over (in the school) I asked all the people to remain, so that we might have a little talk together about the Institution which I hoped would be built during the summer. The Indians, I said, had now transferred the land to us by deed, so that there was nothing to prevent our commencing the buildings at once. It was necessary, however, to consider what children would be received into the Institution when it was completed. Many friends were ready with their money to pay for the support of pupils, but they wanted first of all to know their names and ages, and other particulars. I felt, I said, that this was an important matter, and it was time now for me to ask them whether they were willing to give up their children to be trained in our Institution. I knew that it was a great responsibility for me to undertake the charge of their children; if it were not that I was persuaded that our whole undertaking had been from first to last ordered by God, I should consider it too heavy a burden, but I was sure God would be with us and bless us—it was His work, and not mine. Chief Buhkwujenene replied. He alluded briefly to our visit to England, spoke of the generosity of the English people in contributing, and ended by saying that he should gladly send two of his daughters to our Institution. Chief Little Pine then rose. He addressed himself specially to the women, and told them a great work had been done for their children, and they must make up their minds now to give them up. In a humourous tone, he said, all the *weaned children* must be sent to the Institution at once, and the infants be kept until they were old enough. Their Missionary, he added, seemed to think it would be a heavy burden on him, and so indeed it would be if he were alone: but he was not alone, God would help him, and so it would be light. He concluded by urging on the people to listen to the good counsel they had received. All that had been spoken was truth—it was all truth.

CHAPTER XXI.

THE OPENING OF THE FIRST SHINGWAUK HOME.

ON June 3rd, 1873, the contract for the erection of the new Industrial Home was signed. It was to cost 1550 dollars, and to be completed by August 25th. The specifications showed that it was to be a frame building, having, with the old parsonage, a frontage of 100 feet, two stories high, with verandah in front for each flat; suitable farm buildings were also to be erected on the land in the rear.

It was interesting to us to watch the progress of the work day by day, to see the walls rising up, the partitions made between the rooms, and at length the roof put on and shingled.

The plastering was not yet done when the first batch of children arrived. They came from our old Mission at Sarnia, and were accompanied by Mr. Jacobs. Their names were Mary Jane, Kabaöosa, Mary-Ann Jacobs, Betsey Corning, Eliza Bird, John Rodd, Tommy Winter (who was at Kettle Point); also Nancy Naudee and Jimmy Greenbird, from Walpole Island. It was difficult to find accommodation for them all, as the rooms were not ready; however, we managed to pack them in.

It was just at this time that the district of Algoma, with Parry Sound and Muskoka, was set apart by the Church as a Missionary Diocese, and on the 10th September, 1873, Archdeacon Fauquier, of the Huron Diocese, was elected our first Missionary Bishop. His consecration was appointed to take place October 28th.

And now I must tell about the opening of our Home, which took place on Monday, the 22nd of September.

It was a fine bright day, and preparations began early in the morning with the hoisting of flags, ringing the church bell, and firing of guns. A string of flags—blue, yellow, red, and white—adorned the

face of the building, and a large Union Jack, given by Mrs. Buxton, was hoisted on the centre of the roof. Men on the Reserve met first, early in the morning, for a " clearing bee " on the farm; and at 4 p.m. a general gathering of all the people was appointed to take place at " The Home " for the opening ceremony.

We had at this time the promise of twenty-three

pupils, but only sixteen had as yet arrived—eight boys and eight girls. Six came from Sarnia, two from Walpole Island, two from Manitoulin Island, and six belonged to Garden River. Among the latter were Eliza Pine's little orphan boy Benjamin. They all seemed very happy and contented in their new home. Those who came from a distance had their travelling expenses paid by their band; and we thought, if anything, it was rather an advantage to get them, as their homes were too far off for them to be likely to run away if they became home-sick. Both boys and girls worked very well, helping the matron (Mrs. Shunk) and schoolmaster to get everything ready by 4 p.m. The dining hall was prettily decorated with stag-horn, moss, and flowers, and laid out with tables bearing, on one side of the room, a "heavy dinner" for those who had been toiling at the "Bee," and on the other side a light repast for other visitors. The hall was soon crowded with people, and all came in for some share of the feast. Then we had croquêt and other games in the garden until 6 p.m., when a bell was rung, and all gathered in the hall.

The two Indian Chiefs, Buhkwujjenene and Augustin Shingwauk (Little Pine), Mr. Frost, and myself, sat at a table at one end, with the boys and girls of the Home ranged on our right and left, the rest of the room being occupied by the people.

The opening ceremonies were conducted in a very simple manner, with a short service, a special prayer for the occasion, hymns, and the declaration that the building was now open, and was to be known by the name of "The Shingwauk Industrial Home," Shingwauk (a pine tree) having been the family name of the Garden River Chiefs for several generations back.

Then I invited the whole crowd of people to follow me in order through the building, that they might see every part of it. I went first, with a lamp, and was followed by the Chiefs and all the Indians, and the schoolmaster, with another lamp, brought up the rear. We ascended the boys' staircase, through the master's bedroom into the boys' dormitories, looked into the clothing store well

supplied from English and Canadian Sunday-schools; then down our own staircase, into the dining-room, out again into the hall, through our kitchen and the Institution kitchen, and the matron's sitting-room, into the girl's work-room and dormitories, and so back to the dining-hall. Then all again took their places, and the meeting was continued. I read over the rules which had been placed on boards and hung up in the dining-hall; read over the names of the children already admitted, gave a few particulars about our work, and then invited the Chiefs each to give an address. They spoke very warmly, and expressed themselves as highly gratified with all that had been done and was being done for their advancement, and thanked God that this "big teaching wigwam," which they had so long wished for, was now built and opened for use. We then concluded the meeting with another hymn and the blessing.

I had been very successful in getting support for my Indian children. Several Sunday-schools in Toronto and elsewhere had kindly undertaken the support of individual children, and Tommy and Jimmy were provided for by kind friends in England. We thus had much reason to be hopeful and to thank God.

During the remainder of the week our Indian children attended regularly every day at school.

At last, Saturday night came; tea and prayers were half an hour earlier than on other days. Mr. Frost played the harmonium, and the children sang sweetly "Shall we gather at the river?" Then they had their baths, and all retired to rest, looking forward to a happy day on the morrow, the first Sunday in our new Institution.

CHAPTER XXII.

Fire! Fire!

At 10 o'clock that Saturday night (September 27th) I went my rounds as usual to see that all was well. Earlier in the evening we had fancied that we smelt burning, but it was accounted for by the matron, who said that she had put some old rags into the washhouse stove. Everything seemed to be safe and comfortable, and at 11 p.m. I retired to rest.

About 3 o'clock in the morning Mrs. Wilson and myself were simultaneously awakened by the running to and fro of the boys in the dormitory overhead, and the shouting of the schoolmaster. We were both up in an instant. I lighted a candle, put on a few clothes, and opened the door leading into the nursery. The cause of alarm was immediately apparent. Flames were leaping up at the back of the house, seeming to come from the cellar, which was entered by a staircase from the outside, just under the nurseries. Every one now was crying "Fire!" and all seemed to be rushing about frantically. Mrs. Wilson called to the servants to wrap our children in blankets, and escape with them. I ran from the nursery to the kitchen, where was a door that led out to the back; there I found Cryer and Frost vainly endeavouring to stifle the flames by throwing on buckets of water. It was raining in torrents. Not a soul was at hand to help us. I sent Cryer and Frost to the river for more water. It was pitch dark, and the river a considerable distance off, so that by the time they returned, the flames had made great headway. It was evidently too late to save the building. Mrs. Wilson and the servants had collected the children; I caught up one of them, and we all ran to the church through the vestry. I rang the church bell hard for some minutes; still no one came. The children were wrapped in blankets, all four of them ill with coughs; the youngest, Mabel Laurie, very ill with inflammation of the lungs. I ran back to the washhouse; the flames now were leaping up madly, and lighting all the country round. I collected the Indian children in the garden, and counted them over; two were missing. Frost said he was sure they were all out; but we could not tell. We shouted into the burning building; afterwards we found that they were all right. I ran into my study, keeping my head low to avoid the smoke, unlocked three or four drawers, and rapidly collected important papers; then, half smothered, groped my way back to the hall. Mrs. Wilson had followed me, and held the door closed while I was in to keep the fire from drawing outwards; the staircase was on fire, and my hair and whiskers were singed. All our watches, jewellery, &c., were lost. My wife had collected and put them together in a basket on the floor, but it was too late to save it. Some of the Indians had now arrived, and I told them to save what they could, but every room was full of flame and smoke. The harmonium in the dining-hall might have been saved, but no one thought of it; it had only been brought in the day before, and was a gift from a lady in England. The church was now in danger; it was only 20 feet from the burning building; where should we go? We took up the children, and ran back to the farm buildings. It was still drenching with rain; the fire looked terrible, and we feared it would reach us even here. We must beat another retreat. Should we go to the Jesuit priest? He was a hospitable man, and would surely give us shelter. "Take up the children again," I said, "we must go at once." My wife persisted in carrying little Laurie, the youngest; I took the other little girl, and the servants carried the two boys. Thus we went through the pelting

rain, the women with only shawls wrapped round them; my wife in her dressing-gown and slippers. I hastened on to the priest's house, and after a good deal of loud knocking succeeded in rousing him. He expressed the greatest sympathy, and invited us in. The rain had drenched us to the skin. I left Mrs. Wilson in charge of the priest's housekeeper, and ran back for the other children. If I did give way at all it was just now when, for the moment, I was alone. I felt that all my hopes and prospects were dashed; still I could pray, and God was not far off. I was comforted. Man might fail me, but God would not. If anything, it was good to feel every earthly prop give way, and to cling alone to the Mighty One.

On the road I met the servants with two of the children. The flames were advancing on the barn; they had already seized on some out-buildings which lay between, and a pile of cordwood. Archie, our eldest boy, of four years old, was sitting under the fence, not crying, but a smile was on his lips, his blue eyes gazing calmly on the flames, his sunny locks wet with the falling rain. I took him up, and ran back with him to the priest's house. "Naughty fire to burn down papa's house," he said. "Papa, shall we go away in the big boat now our house is burnt?" Leaving the little fellow safely with his mother, I returned quickly to see after my Indian children. The Indians had already taken some of them away to their houses, and the rest I sent into an empty log house which Shunk had occupied. Then I turned my attention to the church. The people were standing round doing nothing. I saw the church was in imminent danger; part of the bell-tower had caught, and the roof was smoking with the heat. I called aloud to the Indians to bring wet blankets and put them on the roof, then I seized a rail, told some of the Indians to do the same, and together we pushed over the burning end-wall of the doomed building, and it fell with a crash into the glowing embers. Thus the church was saved.

When I got back to the priest's house I found Mrs. Wilson very ill; but the housekeeper, a kind-hearted French woman, was doing all she could for her. The sexton, an Indian, came to know if he should ring the bell for service. I was scarcely aware it was Sunday, but I said, "Yes, and I would come myself." I had no hat, but the priest lent me his fur cap, also his boots. I would not go into the reading-desk, but knelt in the church, and read the Litany. All the people seemed greatly affected. I spoke a few words to them, comparing our position to that of the Israelites when, on setting forth, full of hope and joy, on their road to the Promised Land, found their way suddenly barred before them by the Red Sea. I told them that the events that had happened seemed sad and distressing to us, but who were we that we should understand God's purposes? We must believe that it was all for the best; we must wait on God; He would make the way clear for us. If it were His will, no doubt these ruins would be built up again, and we should all rejoice once more. Buhkwujjenene then said a few words, and spoke very feelingly. When this little service was over, I returned to the priest's house, and sat down at his table to write a telegram. There was telegraphic communication with the outer world through the United States, the wires having been extended to the American Sault only a few months previously; thus I was enabled to telegraph to England. I wrote, "All is burned down; no lives lost; nothing saved." The priest, who had been most kind throughout, sent it for me to the telegraph office, thirteen miles off. He sent also at the same time for the doctor and medicines, and a message to our friends at the Sault telling of our sad plight.

We now determined to go as soon as possible to Collingwood by the steamship *Cumberland*, which was due on her way down. Poor little Laurie was very ill, and we anxiously awaited the arrival of the doctor. During the afternoon, I poked through the ashes with a stick, and found the remains of our watches and two sovereigns welded together. We also collected a quantity of silver, all welded together, scarcely a spoon or fork retaining its shape; still it was valuable, and I disposed of it afterwards in Toronto. Among the chief valuables destroyed were our piano, recently brought from England, the harmonium, a library of 500 volumes, and all our stores for the winter which had just been laid in. The whole loss was estimated at about £1300. The carpenters had only been out a day or two, and I was intending to insure the building the following week.

CHAPTER XXIII.

After the Fire.

Late in the afternoon Dr. King, of the American side, arrived. He was very kind and did all he could both for my suffering wife and our sick child; there seemed but little hope that the latter would live, in her weak state the shock had been too great. After tea I went over to see my poor Indian children. All were lacking in clothing more or less. Jimmy Greenbird, who ran into Frosts' room after the fire began and saved his coat for him, was rolled up in a counterpane. Little Nancy, eleven years old, had her hand to her head and looked ill. She said, "My brain pains me." She seemed inclined to faint, so I took her in my arms and gave her some restorative. All night our little Laurie was very ill, and Mrs. Wilson never slept at all. Next day, Monday, the Indians held a council to hear from me what I proposed to do. They asked me whether I felt "weak or strong about it," whether I would collect money to re-build again, or whether I should give up the Mission. I reminded them of what I had said in the church. I could only wait on God till I saw my way. Some of them said it was unfair to ask me just now when the calamity was but just over, and my wife and child sick; it would be better for them to set to work and try and repair the damages and leave me more time to think: they then talked of putting up a house at once for our school-master, as he would remain and take my place this winter. Old Chief Little Pine, spoke very nicely; addressing me, he said, "The destruction of these buildings and property is not loss. Were you to lose your wife and children it would be loss, for they cannot be replaced. I have just lost a son, and I know what that is." Our friends at the Sault were most kind and sympathising; they sent us a portmanteau full of clothing and food.

One more sad event has to be recorded. Tuesday was a clear cold morning, and the stars were still shining brightly, undimmed as yet by the streaks of dawn in the East, as I wended my way to the church. I was going to toll the bell, for our little daughter Laurie was dead. The soft morning star beamed down upon me as in pity; all was quiet, all looked calm, serene, and peaceful,—the silence only broken by the deep tolling of the bell. The little coffin had to be made in haste, and was only just ready in time, for the steamship *Cumberland* arrived at 10 a.m. My wife was carried on a mattress down to the steamer. The boat could only stay a short time. The servants and the other children were already on board. I gently lifted my child into her last narrow bed, then Cryer and I carried it on board with our hats off. Frost remained behind to take charge of the Mission temporarily. The Indian children who had come from a distance were left with him and the Matron until we could decide what to do. The captain and officers were very kind. When we got to Bruce Mines, I went up to a store to buy a great coat and other necessaries. My wife was still in her dressing gown, being too ill to dress. We had special prayer on board for fine weather, the captain and others joining with us. On reaching Collingwood, we were most kindly received by Dr. and Mrs. Lett. They were greatly distressed to hear of our sad misfortune, and my wife was carried up with the greatest care to their house. They gave up their own bedroom to her on account of its being warm and comfortable, and would not hear of our going elsewhere. Late in the evening a vehicle was engaged, and Dr. Lett, my two little boys, and myself went together to the cemetery which is some distance off—taking the little coffin with us. It was too late to read from the Service-book, but Dr. Lett repeated some portions of the service from memory, and our little girl's body was committed to the ground—"earth to earth, ashes to ashes, dust to dust,—in sure and certain hope of the glorious resurrection."

The telegram announcing our disaster was received at my father's house in England at 8 p.m.

Oct. 1st, three days after it happened, and a reply expressing much sympathy was immediately telegraphed to us. A week later came a letter saying that £250 had already been subscribed towards the rebuilding: this simply in response to the telegram. Very great sympathy was aroused, and letters came pouring in from kind friends both in England and in Canada. By Oct. 16th the "fire fund" in England had reached £518, and this before any letters with details had arrived. Our friends up to that time knew only that "all was burnt down." They were anxiously expecting letters, and hoped to hear that we had at least saved some of our personal property. The following are extracts from some of the earliest letters received in response to the first detailed tidings of our calamity. "Your letter, giving the details of that terrible escape and your great anxiety, only reached us yesterday morning (Oct. 22). It made our hearts bleed for you. But how comforting to know that you were kept in peace, even amid *such* sorrow. I knew you would be helped and comforted, as God's children always are, when their need is the greatest. And now our fears and longings have been greatly relieved by the short telegram which arrived at 4 a.m. to-day. We do indeed rejoice and thank God with you for this great mercy. After your sad account of your dear wife and her falls in escaping we feared much for her, but what a joy to have another living babe in place of the sweet little one whom the Good Shepherd has folded in His own arms. . . . How mysterious it seems that everything, just when completed, should thus in a moment have been destroyed; and then, just when the fire came, that the children should have been so ill: but if trials like these do make us cling the more to the Mighty

One shall it not be well? . . . £550 is now in hand for you, and more keeps coming in."

Another writes:—"I cannot say how we all felt for you in your great trial, such an overwhelming, overpowering misfortune; and then your darling child's death too, it all seems to have come upon you like an avalanche. Well, you have the best comfort. I came upon such a nice verse for you this morning, "David encouraged himself in the Lord, his God."

On the 30th October, a large packing case and bale were despatched from England containing full supplies of clothing and house requisites, books, &c., and many handsome presents from our kind and sympathizing friends.

But besides all this help from England we received also very much sympathy and a great deal of substantial help from our friends in Canada. The very first contribution I received towards rebuilding was from the Methodist minister of the Sault, although I had never made his acquaintance or spoken to him. One lady sold a diamond ring from her finger and sent us the proceeds, and many others helped liberally. Dr. Lett was indefatigable in his exertions for us. The following is from our dear Bishop, who had been elected only a few weeks before the fire occurred and was not yet consecrated.

"My dear Mr. Wilson,—I have only to-day been able to ascertain with any probable certainty where I could hope that a letter, conveying my deep and heartfelt sympathy with you and yours under the late severe visitation which Our Heavenly Father, doubtless for wise and good purposes, has seen fit to bring upon you, might find you. . . . I feel assured that you have gone to the right quarter for comfort and support in the trying hour; and that so doing you have experienced the faithfulness of Him, who hath promised that He will never leave nor forsake such as trust in Him, and have been comforted. If, in the midst of all your cares, you can find time to send me a line, first to tell how your dear partner is—whom I pray may be spared to you—as well as how you are yourself, and then what your plans for the future are, I shall indeed feel greatly obliged. Such trials as these must not discourage us, but rather quicken our exertions and stimulate our zeal. Praying that you may be strengthened and supported in this your hour of need, and realize that it is *good to be afflicted*, believe me to remain your affectionate and sympathizing brother in the Lord, F. D. FAUQUIER."

CHAPTER XXIV.

PROSPECTS OF RE-BUILDING.

"SHINGWAUK—an announcement!" Such was the heading of a communication which appeared in the correspondence columns of the "Church Herald" in the Spring of 1874, between four and five months after our fire,—and it ran thus: "A little more than four months ago the Shingwauk Industrial Home at Garden River was burnt to the ground, and not a vestige of it left. An appeal was then made to Church people of Canada, England, and Ireland to assist in re-building it, and the sum required being £2000; the building to comprise an Industrial School for boys and girls, and principal's residence. I am happy to announce that this sum is, so far as I can ascertain, almost, if not already, secured. From the Canadian Church, 1410 dols.; from Government, 1000 dols.; and the balance from the Old Country. I mention this in no spirit of boastfulness, but in humble gratitude to God the Father and our Lord Jesus Christ, that the Holy Spirit hath thus inclined the hearts of His people to give. All that has been contributed has been 'offertory money' in the truest sense of the word. No expense (beyond printing) has been incurred, and every contribution that has been offered, whether of á hundred pounds or a penny, has I believe been given with a full and grateful heart, as unto God and not as unto men."

It was indeed a very great cause not only for thankfulness, but for deepened faith and more earnest trust in God, the Giver of all good gifts, that a work which had seemed so completely destroyed should thus, in the short space of four and a half months, without any effort being made on my part, be in a fair way towards re-establishment on a larger scale and on a more sure and permanent basis than before. Truly can we say,

> "God moves in a mysterious way
> His wonders to perform."

If only we have faith in God, how much more may be accomplished than we have any idea of. He is *able* to do for us far more than we can either ask or think.

I feel it only right, at this point, to place it on record, as an encouragement to others who would fain trust simply in God, that the effect on myself of that fire—I cannot call it that disastrous fire— was to draw out fresh faith and trust in my heavenly Father. At that time, when every earthly prop seemed to have given way,—when we suspected incendiarism and knew not whom to trust, and my little daughter was dead, and my wife seemed to be dying, and all things seemed to be against me,—I was enabled in that hour of deep trial to look above, to realize that God was my Father—my good Father—who would not let me want; in my helplessness I just cast myself upon Him, and rested on His strong arm. Before, I had often been anxious and had worried myself about the future, but in this my hour of distress I felt very deeply how insecure are all earthly investments, and that as His servants,—" labourers together with God," our work not of earth, but of heaven,—the truest happiness was to depend very simply on our heavenly Father for the supply of all our daily needs.

Certainly it was wonderful how the money came in for re-building our burnt Institution. The English fund kept mounting up. First it was £250; that was a little more than a week after the telegram was received, and before any details had arrived. Eighteen days after the fire it was £518; a week later, £550. In four and a half months it had mounted up to £1500; just double the amount we had collected for the first Institution. And all without any great effort being made. It seemed like a fulfilment of the verse, "The Lord shall fight for you, and ye shall hold your peace."

And now we must return to Collingwood.

Spring has come; the Indian grammar and dictionary are completed, and have been sent to Toronto for publication; the ice is moving out of the bay,—the first steamboat preparing to start northward. We bid adieu to our kind friends, and are off once more to Algoma!

On the second morning we pass the Garden River dock. Our poor Institution is gone; and in its place stands a very desolate-looking frame cottage, with only a door in front, and not a single window facing the river. It has been built on the site of the burnt building, and is occupied by Mr. Frost, the Catechist. The poor old church is standing still, scorched on one side. Some of the Indians are waving to us as we pass;—but we are not going to stop there,—the boat goes gliding on, and an hour later we are landed on the Sault Ste. Marie dock [1].

We had engaged a house for the summer, near the river, and here we took up our residence on the 18th day of May. Early the next morning I started off to look for land whereon to build the new Institution. East, west, and north, high and low, land was looked at, but none seemed sufficiently desirable to choose as a site for the new Shingwauk Home; either it was too near the village, or too far away, or too far from the river, or of too high a price. At length, however, the spot was decided on. One sultry evening, almost the last day of May, my wife and myself sauntered down the road along by the bank of the broad Ste. Marie River, a distance of nearly a mile and a half from the village. Here was a little open clearing, while all around was thick, tangled, almost impenetrable bush, but in front was the beautiful sparkling river, a mile and a half in width, and two pretty green islands just

---

[1] Shortly after this the Rev. P. T. Rowe was appointed by the Bishop missionary to Garden River. It was thought better for many reasons to erect the new Institution at Sault Ste. Marie in preference to Garden River.

in front of us. Cryer, the farm-man, had followed us with a spade, and we got him to turn up the sod in several places that we might see what the soil was like. We decided there and then to make this the site of the Shingwauk Home. The soil indeed was somewhat stony, but the distance from the village was just what we wanted, and the land was cheap (only £1 an acre) and, best of all, it was close to the river, which meant plenty of boating and fishing and swimming for the boys, and skating in winter. We bought ninety acres, but it cost us nothing, as the Municipal Council gave us a bonus of 500 dols. On the 3rd of June (our wedding-day) I selected the spot on which to build, measured it and staked it out, and assisted Cryer to chop out a clearing. The bush was so dense that we could see nothing of the river from where we were working; but after a few days' labour the clearing was extended to the roadway, and we could then see where we were; we made some big fires, and burnt up the brush-wood as fast as we cut it down. On the 24th June the contract was signed, and excavations for the building were commenced.

The first week of June saw the arrival of Bishop Fauquier to take up his residence at Sault Ste. Marie.

The first week of June also saw the first issue of our little Missionary paper, at that time called the "Algoma Quarterly," but now the "Algoma Missionary News."

CHAPTER XXV.

LAYING THE FOUNDATION STONE.

ON Friday, the 31st of July, 1874, the foundation stone of the new Shingwauk Home was laid by the Earl of Dufferin, Governor-General of Canada.

It was fortunate that his Excellency had planned a trip to the Upper Lakes just at this very time. Two days before his arrival a telegram was received from Col. Cumberland, Provincial A.D.C. who was accompanying his lordship—" I have his Excellency's commands to say that it will give him much pleasure to lay the corner-stone of your School on his arrival, which will probably be Friday afternoon." All now was bustle and excitement, and great preparations were made; triumphal arches erected, flag-poles put up and flags hoisted, and a cold collation prepared in the carpenter's shop, which was the only building at present erected. The ladies of Sault Ste. Marie most liberally gave us every assistance, and the "spread" of good things was complimented by the Governor-General, who remarked that he had never before seen a luncheon so tastefully laid out in Canada.

On Friday, at 1 p.m., the steamship *Chicora*, which had been chartered by the vice-regal party, drew up at the Sault dock. The leading inhabitants of the place welcomed his Excellency on landing, and presented him with a loyal address, to which he made a suitable reply. During the procession a salute was fired by a company of volunteers. The guns were two handsome brass field

L

pieces, strongly mounted, bearing the date 1776. An old Highlander who accompanied the party remarked, "Captain Wilson's guns are twa sma' pieces, but they make a tremendous noise;" and certainly the reports, as they followed each other with the utmost regularity, justified the remark.

After some introductions to the Governor-General, he and Lady Dufferin embarked for the Shingwauk Home. They were followed by quite a fleet of other boats, and in due time all landed at our own newly-made dock. Here we met the distinguished party, and accompanied them to the site of the new buildings. Our Bishop being away, the responsibility of the occasion all rested on myself. After a short service, conducted by the two visiting clergymen, Lord Dufferin advanced and gave us the following address:—

"It is with great pleasure that I have taken an humble part in the interesting ceremony of to-day. I am always glad to have an opportunity of showing the sympathy which I feel and the interest which I take in the welfare of our Indian fellow-subjects. We are bound to remember that we are under the very gravest obligations toward them, and that the white race, in entering their country and requiring them to change their aboriginal mode of life, incurs the duty of providing for their future welfare and of taking care that in no respect whatsoever are their circumstances deteriorated by changes which are thus superinduced. It must also be remembered that, although we ourselves have the advantage of living under Parliamentary institutions, and that the humblest person in the land is able to feel that his representative is in a position to plead his cause and watch over his interests in the High Court of the Parliament of the

Dominion, for obvious reasons these advantages have not yet been extended to the Indian population. On that account, therefore, if on no other, we are bound to be very solicitous in our endeavours to advance civilization, to settle the country, and to bring it under cultivation, that we do them no wrong or injury. I must say that no better or surer method could be adopted to secure those results than that which we have now assembled to inaugurate. It is very evident that so great a change as that from the wild life of the hunter to the occupation of the cultivator could scarcely be effected at all, unless those who are thus invited to alter all their habits of thought and life are educated with that intent. For this purpose it is obviously the best method to lay hold of the younger generation, by instructing them in the arts and habits of civilized life, and to put them in a position to join with us on equal terms in our endeavour to build up this great country, so that the various races may be united by common interests and in a common cause. I am happy to think that with this intent there is further joined the interest of religion, which is even a greater and stronger means of cementing the hearts of men together than that of patriotism. But when the two are united and combined, as they are upon this occasion, it is impossible but to anticipate the happiest and most successful results. I can assure you, Mr. Wilson, on behalf of those (and there are, perhaps, many more than you can imagine) who take a deep interest in this work, and on behalf of your Indian friends, that you deserve our heartiest and warmest sympathy. I can only conclude these imperfect observations by saying, on behalf of Lady Dufferin and myself, that we both wish this

Institution and those engaged in promoting it all the success that they themselves could desire."

At the close of this address, I, in a few words, tendered my grateful thanks for the honour his Lordship and Lady Dufferin had conferred on us by paying us this visit and laying the foundation stone of our Institution, and then we repaired for luncheon to the carpenter's shop, which was ornamented with flowers and scarlet bunting.

All passed off most agreeably, and there were many hearty cheers when the little steamboat crossed the great river under a salute to deposit her noble freight on the other side.

Twenty men were at work at the foundations of the new Home the day after this visit, and all went forward with vigour. It may be well here briefly to describe the general plan and appearance of the building. The main building has a frontage of 75 feet, facing the river; it is built of stone, and is three stories high; there was a wing at the eastern extremity, and other additions have been added since; the original cost of the building was 7000 dollars, and the additions have made it worth about 3000 dollars more. At first all was swamp and stumps, but the earth taken from the excavations helped to fill up the low spots, and in time, after considerable labour, the place began to look quite presentable, and a picket fence was put up along the roadway in front. On the side nearest the river were the carpenter's cottage and shop (in one), which have already been mentioned, on the right, and on the left another cottage of the same dimensions, intended at first for an infirmary, but afterwards used as a laundry. These two cottages were quickly erected at a cost of about 600 dollars each, and were found very useful while the larger building was gradually rising into existence; indeed, we were enabled, by making use of these cottages, to re-open the Institution in a small way that very same autumn.

CHAPTER XXVI.

A Trip to Batcheewauning.

BESIDES the Indian Home which was being built I had various other objects to attend to. There were the Garden River Indians to visit from time to time, and I wanted, if possible, to make another trip up Lake Superior. One Indian settlement, about fifty miles up the lake, called Batcheewauning, I had already visited, and the Bishop had consented to my building a school-church there and placing a catechist in charge. So, as soon as the new Institution was fairly started, I arranged to pay a visit to this place, accompanied by Mr. Frost. We took with us a tent and a good supply of provisions, also lesson books and slates, and a voyage of some ten hours brought us to the saw mills, where we were to land. It was a dark night and raining a little. The outline of the saw mill and a cluster of small buildings was just visible. The inhabitants of Batcheewauning consisted of about twelve men and three women—white people, and some sixty or seventy Indians, whose village was six miles off across the bay. We landed our things, a sack of camp kettles and provisions, our bedding and tent.

Jacob, the Indian boy who had come with us, was left in charge, while Frost and I went off to look for a suitable place to camp. The owner of the saw mill directed us to an open spot on the shore, and we bent our steps thitherward ; but after wandering about for some time, searching in vain for a smooth spot, we espied a man approaching with a lantern, and, accosting him, inquired whether all the land around were as rough. "Yes," he replied, "it is only lately cleared, but you will see better in the day-time where to camp,—and to-night you had better turn into the shanty here." To this propostion we agreed, and following our guide, were led into an old log shanty with crevices in its sides and roof. He lighted us a dip, and pointed to an unoccupied corner, where he said we could fix ourselves for the night. The accommodation, certainly, was rude, and the place by no means clean ; yet we were glad of the shelter. We laid our blankets on the floor, and, oiling our faces and necks to keep off the mosquitoes, were soon asleep. At first streak of dawn we awoke. The mosquitoes would not let us rest. They became exceedingly voracious, as always, just at sunrise. It was a fine morning, the water in the bay sparkling in the sunlight, and the thickly wooded mountains looking soft and blue in the far distance. Frost and myself set out again to look for a place to camp. There was not much choice. About eight acres had been roughly cleared around the saw mill, and beyond this on all sides was the thick bush. We overcame the roughness of the ground by borrowing some old boards from the mill, with which we made a floor, and erected our tent over it. Frost kindled a fire, and I made some oatmeal porridge for breakfast, after which we strolled along the

THE OJEBWAY INDIANS.

shore, and were surprised to find an encampment of Indians quite close to us. They belonged to the Indian village six miles off, and were camping here for the summer for the sake of the fishing. They occupied the ordinary conical-shaped wigwams made of poles covered with birch bark, a fire in the middle, and an aperture above for the smoke to escape. We spoke to several, and they said that there were no Indians now in the village; most of them were camping here, and others had gone to Point aux Pins. We told them the object of our visit, which was to ascertain their condition and wants, and, if they appeared desirous to have their children taught, we intended building a school and sending them a teacher in the summer. All to whom we spoke appeared much pleased by this intelligence. Many of them knew me, as I had visited them once before, and they seemed very glad that we could both speak to them in their own language and understand what they said. These people were nearly all Christians. Some had been baptized by Mr. Chance, some by myself, and others by the Methodists; but they had no school for their children and no regular services, and they appeared to be delighted with our proposals to build a school and to send them a teacher. By way of proving their sincerity we invited them to begin sending their children at once to school, and said that while we remained we would teach every day in our camp. This proposal was readily accepted. We commenced at once with twelve children, but found that unfortunately we had come without any alphabet cards. However, this difficulty was soon overcome. We cut the letters of the alphabet out of a newspaper, and pasted them on to a sheet of paper. Mr. Frost taught the children to sing several Indian hymns—"There is a happy land," "Here we suffer grief and pain," &c. They learned the hymns readily, and soon began to join quite nicely in the singing. On Saturday evening we held a council of the people, and I propounded all our plans to them. I told them of the "big teaching wigwam" which we were building of stone at Sault Ste. Marie for Ojebway children from all parts, and told them also of the appointment of a Bishop to reside at the Sault, who would take an interest in them, and would come round in the course of the summer to visit them. Then we spoke of the school-house which we proposed to build for them, and agreed on the spot which seemed to be the most suitable for the site, just at the mouth of Batcheewauning River, near to the Indian village. On Sunday we had three services, and Sunday-school twice. The morning service was in an Indian wigwam, for Indians only. In the afternoon at the saw mill, in English; all the settlers and some Indians attended—in all about thirty. In the evening we held an informal meeting at our own tent. The Indians came together about sun-down, and, it being cold, we all sat round the camp fire. We sang several hymns and I read the latter part of the 1 Thess. iv, dwelling on the subject of the death of Christians as distinguished from that of unbelievers, and then offered prayer, asking God's blessing upon them and their children, and upon Missionary effort among them and their heathen brethren. After the service I was asked to baptize a child, which I did, and then the people returned to their camp.

We chose a very pretty spot for the school; the soil was good, and I purchased 120 acres at 2s. per acre to be the property of the Algoma Diocese; I made a rough plan of the proposed school-house, with rooms for the Catechist overhead,—pointed windows on either side to light both floors, which,

with a bell-tower, would give a church-like look to the little building. The cost I estimated at about 500 dollars. We intended to return to the Sault by steamboat, but none came, so we got some Indians to take us back in their boat,—a man, a boy, and two squaws,—and a leaky old tub it was with old rags stuffed in between the boards. Happily we had fair weather. We camped one night on the road, and got home in about twenty-two hours from the time of starting, after ten days' absence. Very soon after my return I engaged a carpenter, and the following week sent him up with a couple of men to begin erecting the building. Within a month afterwards a Catechist was engaged and placed in charge of the Mission.

CHAPTER XXVII.

The Winter of 1874-5.

By the time winter set in, the walls of the new Shingwauk Home were erected and the roof on, but beyond this nothing could be done until spring. However, we could not wait for the new building to be completed before re-organizing our work. The two frame cottages, already mentioned, had been finished and furnished, and these we intended to utilize for the present. The first pupil to arrive, singularly enough, was named Adam,— Adam Kujoshk, from Walpole Island. We had eighteen pupils altogether, boys and girls; a lady was engaged to act as matron and school teacher; they had lessons and meals in a large common room in one of the cottages, and in this one the matron and the girls resided. The other was occupied by the laundress and the boys. For ourselves we had engaged an old house at the Point, not more than half a mile distant across the bay; so all fitted in very well.

It was a hard winter, but the children kept well, and they had a merry and a happy Christmas. On Christmas morning we all drove in to the Sault to church; such a sleigh load—twenty, I think, altogether,—some sitting, some standing or hanging on, and two brisk ponies to pull. Then there was the Christmas dinner of roast beef and plum pludding, to which all the children did ample justice; and in the evening they came over to our house, and we had a few amusements for them, and sang some Christmas hymns. New Year's night was the time fixed for the Christmas Tree and the prize-giving. Prizes were to be given not only for reading, writing, and arithmetic, but also for laundry work, sewing, baking, cutting wood, carpentering, &c. Such of the children's parents as lived near enough were invited to be present, and a general invitation had been given to our friends at the Sault, so we had a good gathering both of whites and Indians, and the room was crowded. In the building occupied by the matron and girls, coffee and refreshments had been prepared for our guests, and in the other cottage was the Christmas Tree. Passing from one building to the other, a pretty sight was presented by the new Shingwauk Home, illuminated with half-a-dozen candles in each window. The Christmas Tree was loaded with presents, a large proportion of them being gifts from friends both in England and in Canada, and prizes were given to the successful children. We had several Christmas Carols and hymns during the evening, and all passed off pleasantly and happily.

After these festivities were over, I thought the matron needed a rest, for what had been play to others had been in a great measure work and anxiety to her. So I offered to take charge myself while she went to a friend's house for a couple of days.

I was curious to see how the children would manage after three months' training in the ways of the Whites. Our principle was to teach them to *do everything for themselves*, and so we kept no servants; the matron superintended, and every week the children were appointed to their various duties— two cook girls, two laundry girls, two house girls, and so on; and the boys in like manner, some to farm work, some to carrying water, some to chopping wood. Every Saturday the workers received pocket-money from two to five cents each—that is—if they had no bad marks. Well, as I have said, I was curious to see for myself how these rules would work, and how the children would manage, and in no way could I do better than by becoming at once their visitor, teacher, and quasi-matron. Another point, too, I was anxious to ascertain, and that was how "the four cents a meal" plan could be made to answer.

For three months now had these children been fed, and by dint of wonderful care and economy, the matron had managed to keep within the mark. How she could do it had been rather a puzzle to me. The only time that I had undertaken to cater for them, was in the Fall, when I took a number of them down to Garden River, to dig potatoes on our land there, and on that occasion I remember I gave them bread and jam for tea, and found that the jam alone which they devoured cost more than four cents a head, leaving out the bread and the tea.

Well, it was half-past two when I arrived at the cottage. The matron had just left, and it was time to commence afternoon school. The children sat on benches round a long table, Eliza Jane and Betsy, and Benjamin, David, Adam, eighteen of them altogether,—some of them rejoicing in long Indian names as well: Menesenoons, the little warrior; Puhgoonagezhigooqua, hole in the sky;

and so forth. In ages they ranged from the eight-year-old little warrior up to Adam and Alice, the two eldest, who were both turned sixteen. And as regards education, one (*not* the little warrior) was still stumbling over the Alphabet; while one or two who had attended school before they came to us had advanced as far as the Fourth Reader, and were learning English Grammar and Geography.

School was over at 5 p.m., and then the workers fell to their duties, and the non-workers went forth to play. Alice Wawanosh (grand-daughter of the old Chief at Sarnia) was girl monitor for the week, and Mary Jane and 'Hole in the Sky' the cook girls. I was interested to see how very systematically they set to work: Alice got the scales and weighed out the bread half a pound to each child; Mary Jane set the table with a bright array of tin mugs and plates, and 'Hole in the Sky' put the kettle to boil and measured out the tea. Then the bread and butter was cut up, and in a very little time all was ready. At another table a cloth was laid for me, and everything placed ready in the nicest order. When the big bell rang the children all mustered and got themselves tidy, and the small bell was the signal to take their seats. They stood while I said grace, and then quietly and orderly took their evening meal.

After tea came the washing up. Each one, without being told, fell to his or her duty. The boys brought in wood, and filled up the kettle and boiler with water; the girl monitor weighed out the oatmeal for to-morrow's breakfast and handed over to the cook girls, who in their turn carefully stirred it into the big iron pot on the stove. A wise arrangement this to insure breakfast being in good time in the morning, as the porridge has only to be heated up with a little fresh water, and is none the worse.

By seven o'clock everything was in order, books were got out, and the children seated themselves quietly round the table, not for school, but just to amuse themselves, as best they liked. I sat in the Matron's rocking chair by the cook-stove, and was amused to hear them puzzling over the English words, spelling, and helping one another; some of them had copies of my Ojebway grammar, and were teaching themselves the English sentences translated from the Indian.

At half-past seven I suggested they should sing a few hymns before prayers, so the monitor got the hymn books, and they started the tunes themselves, and sang very prettily "Gentle Jesus, meek and mild," "Beautiful River," and "Hark, hark my soul, angelic songs are swelling." Then we had prayers. I read a short passage from the Gospels in English, and explained it in Indian. Kneeling down, they all joined audibly in the general confession and the Lord's prayer. After prayers all went off to bed, the boys over to the Carpenter's Cottage, and the girls into the three dormitories. The monitor and cook girls, however, had to stay up another hour, for bread had been set and was not yet all baked. There was the large wooden kneading trough by the stove, and the scales, and as fast as one batch of bread came out of the oven another went in, one girl cutting the dough, weighing it—four pounds to a loaf—and another making up the bread and placing it in the tins. I think twenty loaves altogether were baked that evening, and very nicely baked too.

John Rodd was the wood-cutter, and his task was to light the fire in the morning. He was early to his work, and by 6 a.m. a bright fire was burning up, lamps were lighted, the bell rung, and soon the occupants of the dormitories began to make their appearance, shivering,—and so indeed was I—for it was a cold morning, twenty degrees below Zero, or thereabouts: the smoke seemed to freeze in the chimney, the window panes were caked with ice, and nearly everything in the house frozen solid. It was just as well that the porridge had been made over-night, even though it was frozen; a little hot water soon brought it to, and it did not take very long to heat up. "Hole in the Sky" stirred it, and kept her fingers warm, and we all huddled round the stove, wishing the wood would stop crackling and smoking, and begin to glow with a red heat.

At last, by seven o'clock, breakfast was ready, the bell rang, and each child sat down to his tin basin of steaming porridge, with a tablespoonful of treacle in the middle. This, with a cup of tea, and a hunch of bread, was their breakfast, and I don't think they fared by any means badly. After breakfast the "workers" went to their house duties, and the boys to their out-door work till half-past nine, when a bell called them to prayers. Then books and slates were got out, and school commenced. All were kept steadily at work till twelve, the cook girls only occasionally getting up to poke the fire or peep into the pots. Dinner was at half-past twelve, pork, beans, turnips, potatoes, and bread; and then there was intermission until half-past two, when they assembled again for school.

Thus all went on very satisfactorily during my two days' visit to this embryo Institution. Merry enough they were, chasing each other about, laughing, talking, and singing, and yet all did their duties regularly and systematically—no jarring or disputes, and no shirking of work, all seemed kind and ready to help one another.

Of the Indian children who were with us that first winter we know the after-record of some. Adam Kujoshk and Alice Wawanosh married May 31st, 1878, and are now living comfortably in Sarnia. Adam is a first-class carpenter, and can command high wages. He was employed in the cabinet-work department, making and fitting the cabins on board the splendid new steamship *United Empire*, which was launched at Sarnia in the Spring of 1883. There is a young Adam, who we hope will one day be a pupil at the Shingwauk Home. Mary-Jane died at her home in Sarnia, trusting in her Saviour. "Hole in the Sky" has been out to service, is a very respectable girl, and gives satisfaction to her employers. David Nahwegahbosh married Sophia Esquimau, another of our pupils, and they are living on the Manitoulin Island. Benjamin Shingwauk, "the Little Warrior," is still with us, studying, and will, we hope, shortly pass the public examination and receive a teacher's certificate. John Rodd died at the Shingwauk in 1877, and was buried in our little cemetery; he died trusting in the Saviour. Joseph Sahgejewh is still with us, working at our sash and door factory, and receiving wages.

CHAPTER XXVIII.

THE NEW SHINGWAUK HOME.

OUR new Shingwauk Home was formally opened on the 2nd of August, 1875, by the Bishop of Huron and the Bishop of Algoma. There was a large attendance, including several friends from other dioceses; the day was very fine, and all passed off most auspiciously. After partaking of a sumptuous repast in the dining-hall, which was beautifully decorated for the occasion, the guests assembled in the school-room for the opening ceremony. A Special Service, prepared for the occasion, was conducted by the Bishop of Algoma, who then offered a few interesting remarks relative to the object of the Institution and the manner in which it had come into existence. He reminded the friends present how the original building had been destroyed by fire six days after its completion, and that the present one, in which they were assembled, had been erected to take its place; that the object was to train young Indians to a Christian and civilized life, and to offer them all the advantages which their white brethren enjoyed. His Lordship then called upon the Bishop of Huron to formally open the building. Bishop Hellmuth, on rising, said that it gave him great pleasure to be present at the opening of this Institution, in which he felt a deep interest. He was persuaded that the true way to do any permanent good to the poor aborigines of this country, was to take their young, and train them. If this had been done forty years ago, he felt assured that there would be many a man now from among them holding high official position in the country. In his own diocese he had at the present time three native Missionaries and a considerable number of native school teachers, male and female, all of whom worked to his entire satisfaction. He trusted that children leaving this building would become centres for the increased spread of Christian truth; and he felt no doubt but that the blessing of God would rest upon a work which had been undertaken in faith and with earnestness of purpose.

The audience then rose, and the Bishop solemnly declared the building open for its intended purpose as an Industrial Home for Indian children, in the name of the Father, and of the Son, and of the Holy Ghost.

After the Doxology had been sung, short addresses were given by Mr. Simpson (formerly Member for the district), and Mr. Dawson, our Parliamentary Representative at Ottawa.

Then, at the Bishop's request, I added a few remarks relative to the system upon which we proposed to carry on the work of the Home. Forty-one children, I said, were at that time present, and we were expecting several more. My experience thus far had been that it was a somewhat difficult matter to train Indians to a civilized life, still I had great hopes that our present undertaking would, under God's blessing, prove successful. The first thing, I felt, was to draw the children around me, and let them feel that I cared for them and really sought their good. I regarded them all as my children. A good proof that I had in some measure gained their affection and confidence was, that many of those who had been with us the previous winter, and had been home during the summer for their holidays, had of their own accord come back again, some of them from a great distance, and all seemed anxious to get on and learn all they could. We keep no servants, I said, but every child is appointed to his or her work, and, as the company might see, wore badges on their arms, indicating their employment for the week. In regard to funds, all was prosperous. Ever since the fire God's blessing had, in a most marked manner, rested upon our work. People had given liberally, without any of the means usually used for raising funds being resorted to. All was paid for, and a little balance in hand.

At the conclusion of the speaking the clerical party retired to disrobe, and then the Bishops, with a number of friends present, were conducted over the various parts of the building. On arriving outside, the Indian children were found drawn up in a line in front of the building, each holding a flag; the National Anthem was sung, and then all marched forward, two and two, in very tolerable order, singing the hymn, "Onward, Christian soldiers." They were followed by the company, and made a complete tour of the grounds. In the evening tea and coffee were served to the assembled guests, and the day's entertainment concluded with a display of fireworks and a bonfire on one of the islands opposite the Institution.

The whole cost of the Institution, with land, cottages, &c., in round numbers, came to £2325.

We soon got into regular working order. School hours were from 9 to 12 in the morning, and from 2.30 to 5 in the afternoon, every day except Saturday. We had fifty pupils, twenty-five boys and twenty-five girls, varying in age from six or seven years up to seventeen. Some of them were very poorly clad when they came to us, and very dirty; and the first thing was to give them a bath and burn all their clothes, and rig them out afresh. It was of course a great change to them to commence regular habits, to run when they heard the bell ring, and do all that they were told; and some of them began to pine under a sense of captivity. Some of them, when home-sick, seemed to lose all control over themselves, and made an unearthly noise; others would watch their opportunity and run away. In the next chapter we shall tell about three run-away boys, and their capture after ten days' absence. On the whole, however, the children seemed to be wonderfully contented and happy, and all went merrily and cheerfully day after day. The fish-boys used to go out after their nets each morning, and bring in plenty of fish; the water-boys had their grey pony, which they called "Muhnedooshish" (Little Evil Spirit), because it had such a bad temper and was always backing up and upsetting the water, instead of going forward with its load. The baker-boys made and baked the bread in the brick oven. The sailor-boys, in their blue serge suits, had charge of *The Missionary*, and did all commissions by water. All were willing to work, and seemed to enjoy their life, and on Saturdays we gave them a few cents pocket-money as an encouragement to good conduct. True, the matron was sometimes at her wit's end, with so many to provide for and such raw young hands to do the work, and it was doubtless a task of considerable difficulty to keep everything in order, and to have meals in time and well cooked, with only these young girls as her assistants, the greater number of whom could scarcely speak a word of

English; and great credit I felt was due to her for her patience with them. However, they really did try to do their best, and were quick enough when they could understand what was wanted of them.

On Sundays the children used all to walk to the Sault to church in the morning, and in the evening we had service in the School-room. On Sunday afternoons there was Sunday school, and on Wednesday and Friday evenings Bible-class. Every morning at prayers the children would repeat a verse of Scripture after me, so as to know it by heart at the end of the week. This plan has been continued uninterruptedly, and the children who have been with us have thus a good store of Scriptural knowledge. They were also taught the Lord's Prayer, the Creed, the Ten Commandments, the Catechism, and the Collects in English, their lessons being of course varied according to their capacities. Our great desire was that they might all prove themselves to be true Christians—servants and soldiers of the Lord Jesus Christ.

The industries which we taught at the first outset were capentering, boot-making, and farming. It was of course a great object to make the children talk English. Twice a week I had an English class, and taught them to repeat English words and sentences, to point to their eyes, nose, ears, &c., and to bring me things I specified. In order to induce them to keep a check upon one another during play-time, I dealt out to each a certain number of buttons of a particular pattern each Saturday, and if any of them heard a companion speak Indian he was to demand a button, and the following Saturday the buttons were exchanged for nuts. We certainly have been very successful in teaching our pupils to talk English. It is an understood thing in the Institution that they must do so, and no Indian is allowed except for about an hour each day. Boys who come to us unable to speak a word of English in September, by the following June can generally manage to make themselves well understood.

For the support of our pupils we looked chiefly to the Canadian Sunday Schools, many of which undertook each a *protegé* at £15 per annum. This would cover the cost of food and clothing for an individual child; and for the general expenses of the Home we depended on the contributions of our friends in England and a grant from the Canadian Government.

CHAPTER XXIX.

Runaway Boys.

One day three boys were missing; nobody could tell what had become of them; the bush was scoured, the roads searched, and messengers despatched to the Sault to try and gain some clue to their whereabouts. After a time it was discovered that some bread and other things were missing, and it became clear that they had decamped. Their home was 300 miles away, and the idea was that they had probably gone to Garden River, about ten miles below us, with the intention of getting on board the first steamboat that might pass, and so get home; so we made up a crew, and late the same evening despatched the schoolmaster and some boys in *The Missionary* to Garden River. They arrived back the next day, bringing word that a boat had been stolen from one of the Indians there during the night, and that, moreover, an Institution button, with "Shingwauk Home, Sault Ste. Marie" imprinted on it, had been picked up in the sand near the place from which the boat was taken.

Nothing more was heard of these boys for ten days, except that one of the steamboats brought a report that they had seen three boys in an open boat near Bruce Mines, and that they had been hailed by them and asked for bread. Ten or eleven days after these boys decamped, we were preparing to start on an expedition up Lake Superior to Batcheewauning; our four sailor boys were ready, dressed in their new blue serge suits and straw hats from England, *The Missionary* was well loaded with camp-kettles, tent, and provisions. We got as far as the Sault, when the wind, which had been favourable, suddenly veered round and blew a heavy gale in our faces, accompanied by thunder and heavy rain. As it was already between 3 and 4 p.m., it was plain we could not start that day, and just at the critical moment word came that those three runaway boys were on an island forty miles below. Our informant was a Garden River Indian. The boys, he said, had turned adrift the boat they escaped in, which was a small one, and had taken a larger one belonging to a Sugar Island Indian. This Indian, finding his boat gone, pursued the boys in his canoe, overtook them, took his boat away from them, and left them alone to their fate on an island.

Shabahgeezhik did not think the boys would be in distress, as there were a few settlers on the island who would feed them if they worked for their board. As soon as we heard this news, we immediately decided to head our boat round and run before the wind down to this island and catch our boys. We just stopped for ten minutes at the Shingwauk in passing, to get a dry coat or two and tell of the change in our plans, and then off we started. It was 5 p.m., and we thought we could make the island that night. Shabahgeezhik went with us as pilot. We ran along at good speed through Hey Lake, across the American channel, in and out among islands. We were soon wet and cold, and it became very dark. Shabahkeezhik steered, and seemed to know well what he was about, but we had some narrow shaves of running into islands, it was so dark. Once or twice we were close upon rocks, but just saved ourselves. We passed through the "Devil's Gap," about as narrow as one of the canal locks, and soon came in sight of the dark line of the Bruce Mines Shore. We had run well; it was only 10 o'clock, and we were nearly there. Once or twice we saw a fire on the lonely, uninhabited shore, where fishing or exploring parties were encamping. It looked cheerful, but we did not stop. Now at length we reached our island, and drew along shore to grope for the dock. There were lights shining from two dwellings—one near the shore, the other upon the hill. Securing our boat, we landed and went up to a log hut. A half-breed woman appeared at the door when we knocked, but she seemed scared when she found there were so many of us. We wanted to find Mr. Marks' house, he being the principal settler on the island. The woman gave us some hurried directions, and then shut and locked the door. We started in search of Mr. Marks' house, which it would seem was up the hill, about a mile distant. After scouring round a little to find the road, we at length hit on a cattle-track which seemed to go in the right direction. But what a track it was! Every step we took it became worse; it led along the side of the hill, through the bushes and tall grass, and under foot slimy sticks and roots spread over a black swamp. For a few steps one would balance one's self, and then down one would go, knee deep in the mire. Always hoping that the road would improve, we persevered for nearly half a mile. But it only got worse, and reluctantly we had to turn back to our starting-point. Then Shabahgeezhik took a run further up the hill to look for another road. In a few minutes he shouted for us to follow, and the track this time led us out just above Mr. Marks' house. It was nearly midnight, but Mr. Marks was standing outside. We told him who we were and what our errand, and he immediately gave the satisfactory information that the boys we wanted were with a half-breed in a shanty just below. He showed us which way to go, and we descended the hill-side in quest of them. Arriving at the shanty, we knocked at the door. A man answered in English, and asked what we wanted. At length the door was cautiously opened. We said that Mr. Marks had told us to come here for three boys who had run away. Upon this the man opened the door, and said, "Yes, the boys were there, and we could take them." A lamp was lighted, and we told the boys, who were lying on the floor and scarcely awake yet, to get up and come along, and then our sailor boys each took charge of one prisoner, and we marched them down to the boat. The boys got the tent up and went to bed with their prisoners, while we accepted the kind hospitality of Mr. and Mrs. Marks, and slept in their house. It was 1 a.m. when we got to bed, and at 4 a.m. we were astir again, and prepared for the start home. The wind was against us, and we had to pull. At 7.30 we went ashore for breakfast. We were very chilly, our things still being wet, and we lighted a large fire and got everything dry. After breakfast we managed to sail a little, tacking against the wind, and by 12.30 p.m. we had made Sugar Island. Here was the American channel, and we resolved to get dinner, and wait for a tow. In this we were very fortunate, for just as we were finishing dinner a propeller came along. We signalled to her, and she very politely shut off steam and gave us a line from her stern. A storm was getting up, rain beginning to fall, and we had to cross Lake George, and had rather a rough time of it, the propeller dragging us forward mercilessly through the crested waves, the spray and foam dashing all over us, so that we shipped a good deal of water and had to bale. Arriving at length opposite the Shingwauk, we got our masts up, and, giving the propeller a wave of hats and a cheer, the tow-line was let go, up went our sails in a trice, and in a few moments more we had arrived at the shore. All the boys were dancing on the dock, greatly edified to see the return of the runaways.

CHAPTER XXX.

Charlie and Ben.

During a short visit which I paid to England in the winter of 1877, the idea was formed of building a separate Home for Indian girls, and now it became necessary to make the project known also in Canada. Accordingly, in the summer vacation of that year I started off, taking with me two little fellows from our Institution—Charlie and Ben, and also a model which I had made of the Shingwauk Home. My object was not so much to collect money as to tell the friends who had been helping us what, by God's help, we had been enabled to do, and what, with His blessing, we still hoped to do.

The first part of the journey was a dash of two miles along a muddy road in a buggy drawn by my spirited little mare " Dolly," with only ten minutes to catch the boat. The next 300 miles were passed on board the steamboat *Ontario*, which, after rather a rough passage, landed us in Sarnia on the night of Tuesday, May 22nd. From Sarnia we took train to Toronto. Here we passed the Queen's birthday, and the boys saw a splendid display of fireworks in the evening. The most remarkable part of the entertainment was a race between a pig and an elephant in mid-air. They were fire balloons shaped like those animals, and it was really very good. On Friday we arrived in Belleville about noon. This was the beginning of our work, and we held our first meeting that evening in the Town Hall. There was a fair attendance, and after the meeting our two boys distributed papers about our Home, and contribution envelopes, which I asked the people to take home with them, and at any future day that they might feel disposed, to put something in and place it on the offertory plate, and it would thus in due time come to us. The envelopes, I should mention, had the following words on them: "Algoma. A contribution to God's work in the Indian Institution at Sault Ste. Marie."

After visiting Brockville, Smith's Falls, and Prescott, we arrived in Ottawa on the 31st. I had here an interview with the Premier in regard to my work among the Indians, which was quite satisfactory, and in the afternoon we went to pay our respects to the Governor-General. Happily his Excellency was at home, and he received the boys very kindly, and showed them through the rooms of Rideau Hall. One thing that he said to them at parting I hope they will always remember. He said, "I hope you boys will grow up to be good Canadians." This just expresses the secret of our work; this is just what we want to do with our Indian boys: to make Canadians of them. When they leave our Institution, instead of returning to their Indian Reserves, to go back to their old way of living, we want them to become apprenticed out to white people, and to become, in fact, Canadians.

At Montreal we had several meetings, and met with many kind friends who evinced great interest in our work.

Early on the morning of June 8th we arrived in Quebec, and found rooms provided for us at the hotel. The Synod of the diocese was sitting, and we received a hearty welcome from the Bishop and many of the clergy whom I knew. In the afternoon I took the boys to the citadel, where they were

THE OJEBWAY INDIANS. 173

greatly pleased to see the soldiers and the big guns; and in the evening we dined at the Bishop's. Both the Bishop and Mrs. Williams have always taken much interest in our work. On Sunday evening I preached at the cathedral. The following day I took my boys over the ocean steamship *Sardinian*, and in the afternoon drove out to visit Wolf's monument and the gaol. The boys each took a copy of the inscription on the monument, and we returned to Mr. Hamilton's for dinner. There was a capital meeting in the National School Hall in the evening. The Bishop of Quebec presided, and nearly all the city clergy were present.

We had not intended to go further east than St. John, N. B., but finding we had a day or two to spare, we resolved to run on into Nova Scotia and visit Halifax. Two telegrams had been despatched, one to Rev. Geo. Hill, rector of St. Paul's, Halifax, to tell of our intended visit, and the other to Montreal in the hope of obtaining a pass from the manager of the line. The application for the pass was happily successful, and after travelling all day and all night and half the next day, we at length reached Halifax, met with a warm reception from Mr. Hill and had a capital meeting. The boys enjoyed themselves immensely, paddling about in the sea water among the limpets and star-fish and sea-weed, and making vain attempts to catch crabs.

Returning by way of New Brunswick, we next visited Fredericton, and were the guests of the Lieutenant Governor, who had most kindly invited us. The Bishop and a large party of clergy and others came to lunch at two p.m., and at four o'clock in the afternoon was a Sunday-school gathering in the school-house, the model was exhibited and I gave an address. After this there was a very pleasing little ceremony at Government House. At Lady Tilley's invitation a number of young girls, members of her Sunday-school class, had met together week after week at Government House and made a variety of articles for sale, then—shortly before our arrival—a bazaar had been held, and the large sum realized of 300 dollars. This sum was presented to me by one of the little girls when they were all assembled in the drawing-room, and is to be applied to the building fund of the Wawanosh Home. The most successful meeting of any that we held took place in the large Temperance Hall. Lady Tilley kindly consented to become one of the patronesses of our Girl's Home. The following day, Wednesday, I called on the Bishop and we spent an hour and a half very pleasantly in examining every part of their beautiful cathedral—the *one* church gem in Canada. The Bishop set to work in his own way to satisfy himself what our boys were good for, and I am glad to say that the result of the examination was satisfactory.

The afternoon of this day, June 26th, we bade farewell to our Fredericton friends and took the train back to St. John. About half an hour before we arrived we received word that a fearful fire was raging, and as we drew near the fated city we found that the report was only too true. The whole city seemed to be in a blaze, the fire appearing to extend fully two miles, even at that early hour, about 6 p.m. Leaving the two boys at the Rev. Mr. Dowling's house, Mr. Dowling and myself started to cross the harbour to try and render some assistance to our friends. We could not take the ferry for the landing stage was on fire, so we hailed a fishing-smack, and landed in Portland. We walked around to the back of the fire; all the principal part of the city was in flames, and everything in wild confusion; hundreds of people, old and young, heavily ladened and hustling each other along, fire engines at every corner, the open places crowded with a motley throng of people with piles of baggage and furniture.

We made our way round to Mrs. Peter's house, where we had been on Saturday; they were all packed up ready to fly, but could not get a team. The flames were fast advancing upon them. The gas works were close by, and it was expected they would blow up every minute. The younger children were already sent off with their nurse. We staid till after midnight, doing what little we could to help, and then returned to Carleton by the suspension bridge, bringing several refugees with us. The following day, Thursday, we drove to the station in St. John by way of the suspension bridge. The city was still on fire and enveloped in smoke. Happily, however, the station was just outside the burnt district, so we bade adieu to our friends and started once more for the west.

After visiting and holding meetings in Toronto, Hamilton, St. Catharines, and elsewhere, we arrived July 4th at Niagara. We were now in the great fruit district of Canada, strawberries, cherries, grapes, apples, plums, peaches, all in the greatest abundance, orchards everywhere, rich luxuriant vines trailing over trellis-work, the earth fairly teeming with plenty. What a contrast to poor Algoma, where we can grow neither apple nor plum and cannot even ripen tomatoes. Nothing delighted our boys more than to sit up in a cherry tree and eat cherries *ad libitum*—such a delicious novelty—and then to be summoned in for a tea of strawberries and cream! In the evening we met

Archdeacon McMurray, who received us warmly. He was the first Missionary at Sault Ste. Marie, more than forty years ago, and very kindly gave us an organ for the Institution. From Niagara, we proceeded by train to Drummondville. The falls of Niagara were scarcely more than a stone's throw from the house, and the following morning as soon as breakfast was over we went to pay them a visit. Grand and impressive as was the sight, I fear that our boys, boylike, were more taken up with a couple of bears in their cages than with that enormous mass of water surging over the rocks, and tumbling 200 feet into the boiling basin of white foam below.

On Friday the 6th we arrived in Brantford and had a meeting in the evening. The following day we walked out to visit the Mohawk Institution, supported by the New England Company; this institution has been, I believe, nearly thirty years in existence, and they have at present thirty-eight boys and forty-two girls. It was strange how shy our boys seemed of the young Mohawks, though making friends so readily with white boys. Mohawks and Ojebways were hereditary enemies, and, in days gone by, used to delight in scalping one another.

Altogether we travelled upwards of 4000 miles, and I calculated that I had addressed about 5500 people at meetings and about 6700 Sunday-school children, besides sermons in churches. Though we made no collections, I nevertheless had handed to me 990 dollars for the Girl's Home Building Fund, and 225 dollars for the Shingwauk.

CHAPTER XXXI.

A Trip up Lake Superior.

It had been arranged that directly the holidays commenced at the Shingwauk Home, the Bishop and myself should start on a Missionary tour up Lake Superior, the plan being simply as follows:— We would take with us our boat, *The Missionary*, five or six Indian boys to man it, and provisions for six or seven weeks. We would first proceed by steamboat 300 miles direct to Prince Arthur's Landing, taking our boat on board; remain there about a week, during which we would pay a visit into the interior; then coast the whole way back, visiting all the Indians along the north shore of the Lake.

When we reached the Landing, the Indian superintendent, to our great satisfaction, invited us to join him in an expedition to the "Height of Land" where he was going to pay the wild Indian tribes their annuity money.

At length after four days we reached the Hudson Bay waters, the Savanne connecting through a long chain of lakes and rivers with Lake Winnipeg. Lac des Milles Lacs, into which we soon entered, is a perfect labyrinth of lakes and islands. Here and there were expectant Indians come out to meet us in their frail bark canoes, and, paddling up alongside, they joined the cluster at our stern. A strange and impressive sight was it when we at length hove in sight of the "Height of Land," a huge rocky eminence like an upturned basin, literally swarming all over with Indians, in every position and every imaginable costume. One solitary wigwam stood at the top and others could just be seen, betraying a considerable village in the rear. A large Union Jack also floated from a mast planted in the rock. There they sat and crouched and smoked, or stood, or leaned with that majestic composure peculiar to the Indian race; while below, on the slippery sides of the rock, tumbled and rolled about their dirty children, or prowled their grim and wolfish-looking dogs. It was a gay holiday time for them all. For three days and three nights pork and flour and tobacco would be flowing freely into their laps from their great and good mother, the Queen; and to every individual, man, woman, and child, yea, to even the papoose of a day old, would be given £1 to spend as they pleased.

We got our tents pitched—the Bishop's and our own—and then went out to survey the scene. A most novel and interesting one indeed it was, wigwams on all sides of us, some of them containing perhaps forty people, others conical, in which were two or three families with a fire common to them all in the middle. In the water near the dock were several boys bathing and diving, as though perfectly in their element. Here and there stalked a stately chief in his scarlet coat, leggings, mocassins, and feathers in his head. The councillors, of which there were three to each band, wore dark coats with scarlet trimmings. But there were more outlandish personages than these to be seen; tall, lank men, with nothing on them but a scarlet blanket wound around the naked body, at times covering the shoulders, at times drawn only around the waist. Nearly all had plaited hair and silver earrings, and many had feathers in their heads, or head-dresses of beads and ribbons. The squaws were dressed much the same as our own Indians, in bodices and skirts, though not quite so tidily. Some of the bead-work worn by the men was very handsome; it consisted mostly of garters below the knee, waistbands and tobacco-pouches worn round the neck and covering the front of the body. They also had their curiously-carved pipes, some of them with stems a yard long, tomahawks, knives, and other appendages.

Soon men and squaws were seen wending their way to their wigwams, bending under the weight of a side of bacon or a bag of flour. Now was a high time of joviality for them all—even the dogs licked their lips and prepared for the feast.

A crowd collected in rear of the Government buildings; and squatting upon mats on the ground were the musicians, three or four in number, beating away vigorously at their very unmusical drums—just the size and shape of a flat cheese, their drumsticks being shaped like a crook. Soon the war-dancers appeared upon the scene, each with a whoop and a flourish of his knife or tomahawk. Conspicuous among them was Blackstone—no longer in European dress, but with legs bare on either side to his hips—a white shirt almost hidden by massive beadwork ornaments, long braided hair, feathers in his head, and his right hand flourishing a bayonet. The dancing consisted in the actors leaping suddenly to their feet with a whoop, and working the whole body convulsively up and down while standing on their toes, without moving from their position, a monotonous whirring sound being kept up all the time, in which the squaws sitting around assisted. This was kept up long enough for me to sketch one man, when with another whoop and a flourish they sank into a squatting position, the drums still going on unceasingly. After a little rest up they got again, and so it kept on for a couple of hours. The proceedings, however, were broken in the middle by a speech from Blackstone.

When it was nearly tea-time I went out to look for my boys, and found Esquimau talking to an old man under a bark shelter with a stick or two burning at their feet; the old man was living quite alone and this was his wigwam, just room for him to lie down and no more. I sent the younger boys to light a fire and get tea ready, and then stayed with Esquimau to talk to the old man. When he found I was going to speak about religion, he called to his children—two men and a squaw—to come and listen. Another man came up, and in rather an officious manner informed me that it was no use for me to talk to the Indians about religion; that they would not listen to me, and did not intend to accept Christianity. The Great Spirit, he continued, has made us all, and he has given one religion to the whites and another to the Indians. He does not wish his red children to accept the white man's religion. I said I was sorry that any of them should think that, but that if any of them did not wish to hear me they could go somewhere else, and I would talk only to the old man. The old man, however, had now changed his mind and said he did not wish to hear me speak. Several others came round and all said that I must not speak to them about Christianity. One said their custom was for any one who wished to speak to them first of all to put down tobacco. This roused me. "No!" I said, "I am not a trader to carry tobacco about. I am working for my Master, the Great Spirit: the Great Spirit has told His followers that when they go out to preach they are not to carry money or anything else with them, they are simply to tell His message; if they are received, it is well, if not, they are to go away from that place and take the message to others." I then said to Esquimau,—"We had better kneel down and ask God to help us, and teach us what to do." So we knelt, and each offered prayer, amid the jeers and interruptions of the Indians. Then I stood out among them and said in a loud voice, " My friends, I have come here to see you about religion, not to buy and sell and trade with you, but to tell you about the Great Spirit who made you. Your Superintendent, Mr. Wright, has come to pay you money, but I have come to speak to you on religion. I have no tobacco, no pork, no money to give you. But I come to tell you of God who made us, and of His Son who came into the world to save us. I have been told that I must not speak, that none of you will listen to me, but I tell you that I will speak to you: God has told me to speak to you, so this evening I will come among you to speak; those that wish to hear me can listen, those who will not hear can keep away."

During tea it was arranged that the Bishop and myself, with the four Indian boys, should go out about sundown and address the people. Before starting we knelt together in the tent, and the Bishop offered up an earnest prayer to God that He would give us grace and wisdom to speak, and incline the hearts of these heathen people to hear and accept His word.

On the road there we were met by Blackstone. He seemed very angry, and said, "I am told that you are going to speak to the people to-night. You must not speak to-night, you must wait until to-morrow." I said, "No, my friend, I must speak to them to-night." "It shall not be," said Blackstone, "you will not be listened to to-night; to-morrow I will let you speak." I pointed to the sky, and said, "The Great Spirit has told me to speak to-night and I must obey the Great Spirit, I cannot obey man about this." Blackstone still refused to allow me to speak, but I was determined, and we went on. We went to the top of the rocky elevation, and immediately began singing a hymn in Indian. Our boys stood out nobly, and sang splendidly. I felt that it required more determination on their part to face the opposition of their own people than for us who were recognised as "black-coats."

The singing attracted a number of people around us, and I spoke out loudly and addressed them. We then sang another hymn suitable for the occasion and the boys sang out lustily, like good soldiers of Christ. After this the Bishop gave a short, but very earnest and pointed address. Then Esquimau spoke very freely and forcibly, urging upon the people to give up their vain customs and accept Christianity. Then we knelt on the bare rock and prayed God to turn the hearts of the people to Himself, after which we left. Quite a number of people had gathered together when the singing commenced, and remained during more than half the time.

July 24.—The next evening we had service again; myself and my four boys standing on the summit of the rocky eminence in the dim twilight, wigwams on all sides below us; a couple of old women cooking at a fire just beside us, and a few straggling Indians or children lying or sitting about. We sang a hymn in Indian at the top of our voices. This brought a great many people out, but not so many as last night. Then I addressed them.

We then sang another hymn, after which Esquimau spoke and urged the people to give up their vain customs and to become Christians; and, after kneeling on the hard rock and offering up an earnest prayer to God to change the hearts of these poor heathen, we departed.

Black clouds had gathered overhead and it was beginning to rain heavily when we sought the shelter of our tent.

July 25.—The day following Blackstone appeared at my tent door. I asked him to come in but he declined. He seemed to be in a better frame of mind, and spoke in friendly terms, telling me all about the journey from here to the place where he generally lives, at the North-west angle about 200 miles distant. I showed him a photograph of the Shingwauk Home, and he asked some questions about it. He stayed some little time, and then said that the Indians were going to hold a council, and left.

About noon the boys returned with a tin pail of raspberries which we stewed and had for dinner. The monotonous sing-song and drum-beating of the Indians had been going on the whole morning in an adjoining wigwam; we were expecting hourly that the council would begin, but Blackstone kept putting it off. I suspected that he intended to have it at our usual time of meeting so as to draw away the people, and so for that reason we had our meeting earlier, about five o'clock. Before starting I called the boys together into the tent, and, after reading a few verses of Scripture, asked them if either of them were inclined to give up the attempt to teach these heathen people; they had been with me through it all, they had seen the reception we had met with, they had acted their part according to the talent committed to them; would they now give it up as hopeless, or would they go with me again to-night? To this they each in turn replied cheerfully and earnestly that they wished to go with me; so we knelt in prayer and asked for God's help and proceeded forth once more to our rocky pulpit. We saw Blackstone going to and fro among the wigwams, and I thought I would ask him once more whether he would give his countenance to our service. So I called to him, "Blackstone, may I speak to you?" "Pahmah, pahmah," (by-and-by, bye-and-bye), was his reply; "I am busy just now.' We waited until he came round again, and as he merely brushed past I resolved to commence at once. We chose a new situation this time, another rocky eminence in the middle of the wigwams. We conducted our little service as usual, and urged upon the people once more to forsake their customs and to accept the crucified Saviour. When I spoke of the Resurrection of Christ on the third day, there was a jeering laugh from some of the Indians which made me think of Acts xvii. 32. Blackstone, as I had expected, commenced his pow-pow or council directly we began our service, and so drew away all the principal men.

But it was time to prepare for our departure.

CHAPTER XXXII.

Coasting and Camping.

QUITE a high sea was running on Thunder Bay when, on *July* 30, having parted with the Bishop, I started off in *The Missionary* with my seven Indian boys. A stiff south-east wind was blowing, and, as our course lay in a southerly direction, we had to tack. We managed, however, to run across Thunder Bay within five or six miles of our point, and then tacked about to reach it; and about three miles further ran into a nice little sheltered bay, where we camped for the night. The boys were merry, and soon had a capital fire blazing up and the camp-pots hissing and bubbling. By eight o'clock supper was ready, and then, after prayer and singing and each one repeating a verse of Scripture around the camp fire, we all turned in for the night, having safely accomplished the first twenty miles of our homeward trip.

It may be well to state at this point, for the information of those who are not acquainted with the topography of Canada, that Lake Superior, upon which we were now sailing, is the largest body of fresh water in the world, the length of it from end to end, by the course which the steamboats take, being 623 miles. The breadth of the lake at the widest point is 160 miles. Its area is fully as large as Ireland, and its mean depth is 1000 feet. The north shore of the lake belongs to the Province of Ontario, is exceedingly wild and rocky, and is inhabited almost exclusively by Indians, with a few Hudson Bay Company's posts at various points on the route. Prince Arthur's Landing is the *only* Canadian town on the north shore, and that has risen into existence only within the last few years. The south shore of Lake Superior borders on the State of Michigan.

July 31.—A dense fog filled the air when we arose early this morning. We waited until eight o'clock to see if it would lift, but as it appeared to have no intention of doing so, we started off, myself steering and the boys rowing. With a good compass, we steered our course straight into Silver Islet. We landed on the main shore, and spent half an hour viewing the silver stamping mills. The fog was now clearing, and we proceeded to cross Black Bay. This was a wide stretch, and we had to pull as there was no wind. After this, we got into a narrow channel studded with islands; then were out on the open lake again, a heavy swell rolling in and breaking on reefs near the shore. About five p m. we came off Cape Magnet, and soon after reached a snug little bay, where we camped for the night.

After two more days sailing, we got into Neepigon, and found the Bishop (who had come on the *Manitoba*) waiting for us. The Bishop had his tent pitched on the shore, and had been cooking for himself in two little bright tin pots. We were all wet and cold, and as quickly as possible our two tents were up and a large camp-fire built, over which were soon hissing three ugly black kettles — one with water for the tea, another with potatoes, another with rice and currants—while the Bishop's

little kettle hung meekly by, at one end of the horizontal stick, and soon lost its brightness under the unwonted heat of the fire.

At 8.30 we all gathered for prayer, and then went to rest. The total distance we had come, since leaving Prince Arthur's landing, was about 100 miles.

We passed a quiet Sunday in our camp at Red Rock. No Indians came round, but we had a little service for ourselves under an awning. In the afternoon our boys gathered for Sunday-school, and the Bishop examined them in the Scriptures and Catechism.

Aug. 5.—We had intended to be up and preparing for our trip to Lake Neepigon at five a.m., but heavy rain caused us to prolong our slumbers, and we did not breakfast until 7.30 a.m. By this time, however, the weather was clearing, and we determined on making a start. There was plenty to do. We had a trip of 200 miles before us and expected to be away about ten days. All the things in *The Missionary* that were not wanted were packed away in Mr. McLellan's storehouse; provisions were given out sufficient to last the three boys who were to remain behind, and supplies put up for the travelling party. Then—about ten a.m.—the large canoe which we had hired was brought round; Uhbesekun, our guide, put in his appearance; portage straps were brought out, the packs made ready, and all placed on board. The Bishop and myself walked across the portage, about three-quarters of a mile in length, while Uhbesekun and the boys propelled the loaded canoe up the rapids with poles.

CHAPTER XXXIII.

Up the Neepigon River.

Five miles of paddling above the rapids brought us to the mouth of the river Neepigon, a rapid stream about 500 yards in width; we had to keep close to shore in order to avoid the current.

Our canoe was about 20 feet in length, and weighed perhaps 150 lbs., she sat as light as a feather upon the water, and the least movement on the part of any of the party tipped it over to one side. The paddlers sat on the cross bars—about two inches wide, Uhbesekun in the bows, then Joseph, the Bishop and myself, Jimmy and William, and Esquimau in the stern, six paddles in all, and we travelled at the rate of from four to six miles an hour.

About 1.30 p.m. rain began to fall, and the clouds threatened a storm. We paddled on fast to a convenient landing-place, and then went ashore for dinner, which we partook of under the tent, the rain pelting down in torrents. However, it was merely a thunder-shower, and in the course of an hour we were able to proceed.

By four o'clock we had reached our first long portage—three miles in length—and now began the tug of war. Esquimau and Uhbesekun got the huge canoe mounted on their shoulders—one at either end of it—keeping it in its position by ropes which they held as they walked, with their arms outstretched. Then followed Joseph with the bag of flour (70 lb.) carried by a portage strap, placed in true Indian style round his forehead. Then started Jimmy with the tent, blankets, axe, and gun, and the Bishop with his bundle of wraps hung on his umbrella. William remained behind with me while I made a sketch. There was no great hurry for us, as the canoe-bearers would have to return again to take the remainder of the things. William's pack consisted of my camp-bed, blankets, mat, coats, &c., and I had the Bishop's valise and some coats. The portage track was narrow, raspberry canes and high grass almost hiding the path; up hill and down hill, and across a creek. We soon met the canoe-bearers going back for their second load, and a little further on was Joseph, who had deposited his flour and come back to meet us.

The tents were already pitched when we reached the end of our tramp on the shores of Lake Jessie,

and soon our cook was at work baking bread and frying pork for our evening meal.

We were all tired, and went to bed about 9 o'clock, after uniting together in singing and prayer under the open vault of heaven. "Sweet hour of prayer, sweet hour of prayer, That calls me from a world of care," was the hymn we sung. William shared my tent with me, and the rest of the boys, with Uhbesekun, slept under the canoe.

The next morning was bright, but with a head-wind, we made slow progress. We accomplished twelve miles across Lakes Jessie and Maria, and pulled up for dinner at Split Rock portage. Here was some of the grandest scenery we had yet witnessed—high, towering rocks, their crests clad with fir and birch-trees, the rapids rushing in a white foaming torrent over the rocks, in two rushing, roaring streams, divided one from the other by a high, precipitous, rocky island. I made a sketch, and we had dinner, and then, having accomplished the portage once more, started paddling. It was not far to go this time. In half an hour we had reached Bland portage, and everything again had to be unladen and carried. Soon we were in the canoe again heading for the opposite shore, with a new set of rapids on our right. Now for some stiff work again, a long portage of about two-and-a-half miles. We each took our packs and toiled away, getting into camp about 6 p.m.

We were rather disappointed with the appearance of Lake Neepigon, with its large unbroken line of horizon, land being almost too distant to be visible. Our baggage was deposited on the face of a great slippery rock, sloping down gradually into the deep water of the lake. A favourable breeze was blowing, and as soon as we had dinner our blanket sail was rigged up. When we were well out into the lake we found quite a high sea running, and our canoe shipped water. Still we kept on, and made about twenty miles before we put into an island for the night at 7.30 p.m.

A disappointment awaited us next morning. A strong head-wind was blowing. We started at 8 a.m., and made about twelve miles. It was very rough, and the waves dashed over the prow of our frail canoe. We went in to an island for dinner, and, the wind increasing, we were obliged to remain there for the rest of the day. All our baking-powder was gone, and we were reduced to "grease bread," i.e., flat cakes of flour and water fried in pork fat. They make a good substitute for bread, but are rather greasy. Joseph had shot a brace of ducks in the morning before coming away, and one of them we had for supper; which, with some potted beef and tea in a tin basin, made very good fare!

August 9th.—We packed up, got all on board, and started precisely at 6.30. It was a head-wind and a high sea still, so we proceeded only about one mile to another island, and then pulled in to have breakfast and wait until the wind went down. At 1 p.m. we made a start, and ran about five miles to another island. After running twelve miles more we put in for supper. We calculated we had come fifty miles on the lake, and had twenty miles more to go. The direct course was sixty-five miles, but we had lost way by going into the bays.

August 10th.—We stopped two hours on the island where we landed for supper last night, and then—it being bright moonlight, and the wind having calmed down, we started again on a twenty mile stretch, determined, if possible, to reach the H. B. C. Post at the head of Lake Neepigon before midnight.

The Bishop settled himself down in the bottom of the canoe, and Uhbesekun, the four boys and myself, plied vigorously at our paddles—forty-two strokes per minute. It was a glorious night, and the keen air put fresh strength into our muscles, so that we kept on untiringly for nearly three hours.

Just at 11 o'clock we came underneath a stupendous cliff, its dark, rugged face glittering in the moonlight, extending far up towards the sky above us, with a few ragged fir trees crowning its summit. It was the grandest scenery we had seen yet. Our

voices echoed as we passed beneath it, and we heard afterwards that it was called Echo Rock. After passing the cliff, another mile or so brought us to the Post. We had some difficulty in finding a camping ground in the dark. The shore was rocky, and we had to cut out a place in the thick bush on which to pitch our tents. The boys made up a large fire, which was grateful in the chill night air, and soon we had the pot boiling for tea. It was 1.30 a.m. when we got to bed, well tired after our long paddle of seventy miles across the lake.

Next morning the Bishop was the first one astir. About 8 a.m. I got up and went with Uhbesekun to H. B. Co.'s store to buy baking-powder and sugar, both of which we had run out of. Prices are high here, flour is 6d. a pound—at the Sault it is only 1½d. Our cook had only just woke up, and was rubbing his eyes when we got back. We were glad to get "spider-bread" again (bread baked in a spider or frying-pan) instead of grease bread. Several Indians came round. I had a very interesting talk with a chief this morning. He and another man came over in a canoe from an island close by, and Esquimau and myself talked to them as they sat floating on the water, keeping the canoe off the rocks with their paddles. The chief was certainly the most intelligent Indian we had yet met with on our travels. He was greatly interested in hearing about the Shingwauk Home, and said that if he had a son young enough to go he would send him, but his children were all either grown up or dead.

We felt very thankful thus to meet one at length who will listen, and who seems anxious for the improvement of his people. The old man's way of speaking reminds me very much of "Little Pine" of Garden River, and he appears to be a man of much the same stamp. Just after this a couple of young boys visited our camp. One of them was a half-breed. They carried bows and arrows, and were shooting squirrels. We gave them an alphabet card. Most of the Indians just round the Post are Roman Catholics, but those scattered over the lake, about 500 in number, are nearly all pagans. The name of the chief with whom we talked this morning is David Winchaub (Bowstring).

We had tea about 7 o'clock, and then put our canoe in the water and paddled over to the island to visit our friend the chief. He was sitting cross-legged in a large tent, his summer residence, cooler probably than a wigwam. Only Esquimau and Joseph were with me. We entered the chief's tent and soon got into conversation with him.

I asked him if he would like me to relate to him the history of Little Pine's conversion to Christianity. He said yes, and listened very attentively, several times uttering ejaculations, as I recounted to him how bewildered Little Pine had been about the many religions offered to him when he was still a pagan some forty years ago; how he and his father and other Indians made a journey of 300 miles in a canoe, and then walked another 100 miles till they got to Toronto; how they went to visit the Great Chief, Sir John Colborne, and asked his advice as to what they should do about religion, and how Sir John Colborne said to them, "This country belongs to the Queen. I belong to the Queen's Church, and I think all you Indians, who are so loyal, ought to belong to the Queen's Church too." And then, how Little Pine and his party returned to Garden River, and ever since that time had been faithful members of the Church of England.

The Chief then made some remarks expressing

his approval of what we had told him, and said he quite understood all that we meant.

I then asked him if he would like me to tell him what was written in God's book, the Bible. There was only one Bible. French Christians and English Christians were the same in that,—they had only one Bible. He would see from what I would tell him whether it was the same as what he had been taught. He said he was willing to hear, and asked me to proceed. As he was rather deaf, and I wanted him thoroughly to understand, I asked Esquimau to interpret what I said instead of speaking to him myself. As I dwelt on the universal sinfulness of mankind, and urged that there was not a single one free from sin, the Chief said emphatically, "Kagat, kagat, kagat, kagat! me suh goo azhewabuk!" (Truly, truly, truly, truly, it is indeed so!) The boys and myself then knelt and offered up prayer to God for this poor, ignorant, yet eagerly-listening chief, and for his people, that they might be taught the true way to life and eternal happiness. It was 9.30 p.m. when we paddled back to our camp. We met as usual around the camp fire, and each one repeated a verse of Scripture; then we knelt in the shade of the dark bush, with the ripple of the water in our ears, and God's heaven lighted up by His silvery moon, nearly at its full, and offered up our confessions, and prayers, and praises to Almighty God before retiring to rest.

Sunday, August 11*th.*—While I was dressing, William came to say that a squaw had come in a canoe with fish to sell. I said, "No, we do not buy fish on Sunday." So he gave her a piece of bread and sent her away. We had arranged with the Chief to hold a short service in the afternoon at his camp, so we passed the morning quietly among ourselves, reading the first part of the Church prayers, chanting the Psalms, and one lesson, and then the Bishop taught and catechised the boys from the Gospel for the day (Matt. vii. 15).

In the afternoon, about 4 p m., we put our canoe

in the water, and leaving our pagan guide to take care of the tents, the Bishop, four boys, and myself, paddled across the water to Winchaub's camp. After waiting some little time, about sixteen or seventeen people gathered together; being Roman

Catholics, the Bishop thought it best not to attempt a service, but merely to address them on the object of our visit. So, after shaking hands with the Chief, the Bishop began. He spoke first of man's sin and the love of God in preparing a way of salvation for us by the sacrifice of His own Son. Then he spoke of the uselessness of mere formal religion, and that we must give our hearts to God. The Bible, he said, teaches us to care for and to do good to one another. Then he referred to our Industrial Home at Sault Ste. Marie, and after urging the people to send their children to it, left it to me to give a detailed account of the work of the Home. The Indians listened attentively to all we said, and the Chief thanked the Bishop, and said that he and the other men would talk together about what they had heard, and later in the evening he would come over and give the Bishop their answer.

CHAPTER XXXIV.

Thirty Years waiting for a Missionary.

At 8 p.m. Chief Winchaub came over, and having had a friendly cup of tea, he delivered his promised answer.—The Indians, he said, approved all that we had said ; they were glad to see us, and that we had built this big teaching wigwam for Indian boys, they would like to have their children educated, but most of them thought it was too far to send their children. He, for his part, if he had a child, would send him, and another man was willing to send his little boy when older, at present he was too young. We asked him about one promising-looking lad we had seen, the dark-eyed boy with the bow and arrows. The Chief said he had spoken to that boy's father, but he was not willing to send him, it was too far, and he would never know how it fared with him.

The Chief then said he had one other thing he wished to speak about,—there was one band of Indians on the lake, not belonging to him, who, he understood, wished to embrace Christianity and become members of the Church of England. At the time of the great council at Sault Ste. Marie, thirty years ago, the great White Chief had told them that they should have a Missionary of the English Church, and they had been waiting for him ever since. After telling us this he bade us adieu and left.

We had already gone to bed, in preparation for an early start in the morning, and I was lying awake, when my attention was attracted by the splash of paddles and an animated conversation going on upon the water.

Esquimau came to my tent and said, " One of those men that the Chief was talking about has just arrived, and he has two boys with him." I said to William, "This is God's doing," and we both got up and went out to see the man; the Bishop also got up and came out. It was a most interesting interview. We stirred up the dying embers of the camp fire and sat around it on logs. This man, whose name we found was Mesten, had travelled about forty miles, not knowing that we were here till he met Esquimau. He said that he and his people, though at present pagans, were prepared to accept the English religion. Their former chief, who was now dead, had told them to do so thirty years ago. He had waited for a Missionary to come until he died, and since then they had been waiting on year after year; they would not accept the French religion, but were waiting for an English Black-coat to come and teach them. He did not know how many they were in number,

but he thought about a hundred; our guide, Uhbesekun, he said, was one of their number. We then made inquiries as to their location, and found it would take us about ten miles out of our way to visit them. The Bishop was so impressed with the evident leading of God's Providence in the matter that even, though it might cause some alteration in our plans, we determined to pay them a visit.

August 12*th*.—Uhbesekun was commissioned to wake everyone at half-past four, but I was the first to wake, and sent William to arouse the others. A head-wind was blowing, so we had to paddle and row hard; we accomplished about thirty miles in seven consecutive hours. We had dinner on a rocky island, and then five or six miles more brought us to the Indian encampment in Chief's Bay. There were only two wigwams visible, with six or seven people in each, a few canoes on the shore, and seven or eight large dogs prowling about. After introducing ourselves to the men and telling them the object of our visit, we paddled on about a mile further to deposit our baggage at the portage, and left two boys and the guide to light a fire and erect the tents, and then the Bishop, Joseph, William, and myself, returned to the Indian camp. The men were away when we got there, so I sat down and made a sketch of the camp. and our boys showed the photograph of the Shingwauk Home to the women, and told them all about it. By this time the men had returned, a fish-box was brought for the "Big black-coat" to sit on, and a tub turned up for me, and then the pow-wow began.

The Bishop briefly related what had led us to visit them, how one of their number had fallen in with us the night before, and had told us that they were desirous of embracing the English religion, and so we had come on purpose to see them.

There were two principal men listening to us, and they several times expressed their approval as the Bishop proceeded. One of them then replied at length. He said, "Thirty years ago all the Indian Chiefs were called together at the Rapids (Sault Ste. Marie) to meet the Great White Chief in order to make a treaty with him about surrendering their lands to the Queen. My father was chief at that time; his name was Muhnedooshans. The Great White Chief (Sir John Robinson) made a treaty with us. We were each to receive £6 a year as an annuity. My father often spoke to us about it when he was alive. My eldest brother is now our chief; his name is Cheyadah. The chieftainship has been in our family for many generations past. We still carry out the precepts of our father; we do not do as the other Indians do. The Great White Chief gave my father a paper which showed the boundaries of the land set apart for our use by the Queen. My eldest brother now has this paper. My father said to us, 'Do not travel about all the time as the other Indians do, but settle upon this land and farm like the white people do.' We obey the precepts of our father. We have already cleared some land, and every year we plant potatoes. We cannot do much more than this until we have some one to teach us. We have built also three log-houses like the white people. Some of us live in these houses in the winter time. Our land is about four miles in extent. At present it is our fishing season, so we are scattered about fishing, and live in wigwams as you see us now. This is how we gain our living. Another thing that the Great White Chief said to my father was, that we should not join the French religion, but he would send us an English black-coat to teach us. So every year my father was waiting for the English teacher to come; he waited on in vain, year after year, and died a pagan. His last words to us were that we should still wait for an English teacher to come, and that when he came we must receive him well and ask him to open a school for our children to be taught. He also told us never to sell our land to the white people, but always to keep it, and not to scatter about, but to keep together. Thus to this present day have we kept to the precepts of our father, and we now welcome you as the English teachers that our father told us to look for."

The Bishop then spoke again, and told them that he felt most thankful in his heart to hear their words; he was very thankful that the Great Spirit had directed his steps to come and see them. He had it in his heart to do all he could for them; he was sorry that he could not at once send them a teacher; that was impossible for the present. All that he could offer was to take one or two of their boys into our Institution at Sault Ste. Marie. Then, at the Bishop's request, I gave the people a full account of the origin and history of our Shingwauk Home, much the same as I had said to Chief Winchaub the night before. They seemed much interested, though afraid to send any children on account of the great distance.

After this the conversation became general. They told us their names; they said they were very thankful we had come to see them; they knew the white man was right about religion, for he knew everything, their knives and axes and clothing were all made by white men; Indians were poor and ignorant, and needed to be taught. They had almost given up looking for a Missionary. When they went to the Hudson Bay Post in the spring, they were told they had better join the Roman Catholics, but they said, No, they would still wait, and they were glad now that they had done so. I then made a list of the heads of families and the number belonging to each, the total being about seventy. We showed them a hymn-book printed in Indian at the Shingwauk Home, which interested them greatly, though at first they held it upside down. Then I showed them the Indian Testament, and told them this was the Book that God had given to us. They handled it very reverently, and answered readily in the affirmative when asked if they would like to hear some of the words it contained. I read part of the 8th chapter of St. Mark, about the feeding of the four thousand, the curing of the blind man, and our Lord's words about the worth of the soul. The people listened most intently, indicating their wonderment by suppressed ejaculations as I read anything that especially struck them, such, for instance, as the fact that 4000 men were fed with the loaves and fishes; but what produced the most intense attention was the account of our Lord's mockery, Crucifixion, and Resurrection. Their sympathy with the suffering Saviour was most marked, and their simple astonishment most evident when I came to the part about the stone rolled away and the angels telling the women that Jesus was risen from the dead.

When we were preparing to go back to our camp, Oshkahpuhkeda said to me, " Well, if my son is not too big, you may take him with you; I know I shall be sad without him, I shall weep often for him, but I want him to be taught, and I will try to control myself until he returns to see me next summer." I said I should be very glad to take the boy, and would treat him as my son, and I would write to the Hudson Bay Company's agent at Red Rock, that through him he might hear how his son fared, and next summer his boy should go back to him, and he need not send him again unless he wished. I also asked him whether he would be willing that the lad should be baptized after he had received instruction. "Yes, yes," he said, "that is what I wish; I wish my son to be educated and brought up as a Christian. My wife," he continued, "is dead; I also have a sickness working in my body—perhaps I shall not live long. If I die, I wish you to take all my children: this boy who is going with you, his brother whom you saw with Meshen last night, this little girl sitting here (about ten years old), and that papoose,—you may have them all and bring them up as Christians.

We thought it would be better to take the younger of the two boys, if Meshen (with whom he had gone) should get back in time, and to this the father also agreed.

CHAPTER XXXV.

The Pagan Boy—Ningwinnena.

WE returned with thankful hearts to our camp. The Bishop was much impressed, and said it reminded him of Cornelius, who was waiting, prepared for the visit of the Apostle Peter; and for my part I thought of Jonadab, the son of Rechab, whose followers carried out to the letter the precepts of their father.

At our meeting for prayer that evening I said to Uhbesekun, "I hear that you belong to these people whom we have been talking to. Will you not join us to-night in our prayers?" So Uhbesekun, instead of going away, as had been his custom, remained with us, wrapped in his blanket on the ground near the camp fire, and when we knelt for prayer he also turned over with his face toward the earth.

Oshkahpuhkeda came over in good time the next day, according to promise, with his two boys. The younger one was to go with us. His name is Ningwin-ne-na, and he is a quiet, gentle lad of thirteen or fourteen. The father repeated his wish that we should take all his children in the event of his death, and took an affectionate leave of his son. "I know I shall lie awake at night and grieve the loss of my boy," he said, "we Indians cannot bear to be parted from our children, but it is right that he should go. If my heart is too heavy for me to bear, I shall come to Red Rock and get on the Fire Ship and come to see him." I took the boy by the hand and said, "Ningwinnena shall be my son while he is away from you; I will take great care of him." The Bishop also said, "We will take good care of your son, and shall hope to come and see you again." Then Ningwinnena followed me along the portage track.

Arriving once more on the shore of the lake, we found a favourable wind blowing, and put up a blanket for a sail. We had thirty miles to go to bring us to Flat Rock, where we should leave the lake and make our first portage inland. We reached it at five minutes to four, the portage occupied fifty minutes, and soon we were launched once more on Sturgeon Lake. A heavy thunderstorm came on, and continued during the time we wended our way through the narrow, stony creek which connects Sturgeon Lake with the river Neepigon. The Bishop and myself sat in the canoe with our mackintoshes on while the boys waded along knee deep in the water, and twice we had to get out and pick our way along the stepping stones as there was not water enough for the canoe. By-and-bye we emerged on the broad Neepigon river, and its swift current now bore us quickly along upon

our course to Long Pine portage, where we were to camp for the night. It had now ceased raining; it was 7.30 p.m., and we had travelled forty miles. The tents were pitched, a fire lighted, supper consumed, prayers round the camp-fire as usual, the new boy Ningwinnena joining with us, and then we retired for the night, three boys and the guide under the canoe, and myself and two boys in the tent.

August 14*th*.—Esquimau came to call up the cook

at 4 a.m. He and Uhbesekun were to carry the canoe across the portage, and return here for breakfast before conveying the remainder of the baggage, hence the early start. We had only twenty miles more to go, and expected to reach Reed Rock in the evening, which was according to the programme we had made before starting.

Ningwinnena seems to be a very nice boy, and quick at taking things in. He has that gentleness of disposition peculiar to savage life, and follows me about like a faithful hound. Last night I gave him his first lesson in the alphabet, and I never saw any boy make such rapid progress; he could say the alphabet through in half-an-hour, although at first not knowing A from B, and a little while after he was spelling and reading such short words as dog, cat, man, fish. He must come of a good stock. He was also most handy in putting up my tent last night, and rolling up my camp bed this morning, seeming to take in at once the right way to do things.

The day has passed, and we are once more back at our Neepigon encampment, having arrived in the middle of pouring rain at 5.10 p.m. The three boys were very pleased to see us back, and we went up to Mr. McLellan's house for supper. He has been most kind in supplying us with milk and fresh butter.

August 16*th*.—The morning opened with a heavy mist, threatening clouds and wind. Hoping for a change for the better, we took down our tents, and by 9 a.m. all was packed on board *The Missionary*,—then, as was our custom, the boys gathered in a semicircle, a hymn was sung, a portion of Scripture read, and prayer offered, Ningwinnena standing beside me and looking curiously at my book as I read. By the time we started, the wind had become favourable and we made a splendid run, getting into Pugwash Bay at 5.30 p.m. Eight or ten birch bark canoes on the shore told us the whereabouts of the Indians, though no wigwams were visible, the bush being so thick; as we neared the shore, the people began to show themselves, men, women, and children starting up one after another from

amid the dense foliage and gazing at us with curious eyes. There were about seventy people, though nearly half of them were away. Some had been baptized by the Jesuits, others were pagans. After ascertaining these facts we paddled along the shore a little way to a sandy beach, where we made our camp. Our three tents were pitched in the thick of the bush like the Indians, and a huge fire lighted in the middle as the weather had become autumnal and chilly.

These poor people seem to have nothing to eat as a rule except fish and small animals; and they sat and lay around like half-starved dogs while we partook of our evening meal. Two or three of them brought raspberries for which we gave them bread in exchange, and we invited one man, who seemed to be something of a chief among them, to take supper with the boys. These Indians are of a very low type, and are very dirty, appearing to have no idea of anything beyond pork and flour.

I went to see an old man who had been baptized about a year ago by the Roman Catholics, and read the Bible to him. His wife was still a pagan, but they both listened attentively while I read and seemed glad to be visited.

August 19*th*.—By 8.15 a.m. we were fairly out on the bay. I steered and the boys rowed till the wind being favourable, we hoisted our sails and made a good start, winding our way for some miles among islands, and then coming out on the open lake. The wind fell, and the last part of the way we had to row, which made us late in getting to Pic Island,—and a hard matter indeed it was to get in. In the dim twilight we could see nothing but high, forbidding rocks, with the dark rippling waves lapping their sides. Being on the side of the island exposed to the lake, we could not think of attempting to land until we should find a secure harbour for our boat, for a sudden storm rising in the night would knock her to pieces on such a coast. At length, groping about among the rocks, we espied a crevice into which it appeared *The Missionary* would just fit. But, oh! what a place for the night! High, slippery rocks, piled about us by some giant hand, no wood for a fire, no grass, no place for a camp—nothing but sharp ledges and points of rocks.

The boys clambered about with their shoeless feet like cats, and we heard them shouting,—"This is where I am going to sleep! This is where I shall sleep!" The Bishop groaned and said, "I shall remain on the boat."

I, for my part, followed the boys, and presently found a sort of small cavern under a ledge of rock, into which I had my camp-bed carried, and having lighted a candle, sent Esquimau to bring the Bishop.

It was really most comfortable, and, moreover, in the corner of the cavern we found a dry log, probably washed there by the waves in a storm; and with this log we lighted a fire and made some tea, and so—after all—we had quite a cosy time of it.

August 20th.—We all slept sweetly till about 5 a.m., when I think we awoke simultaneously; at any rate we were all on the stir soon after that hour. And now we were hungry, and there was no bread, no fire, and no wood, and fourteen miles to get to the mainland, and a head-wind. What was to be done? By the kindly light of day we discovered that our position was not so distressing as we had at first imagined. A little way over the rocks was a shore with drift-wood lying on it, our cook was despatched with the frying-pan and his bag of flour, and after all we did famously.

Before starting off we joined in repeating the morning psalms. We had a hard pull against a steady head-wind, and could only make two miles an hour, so that it was a little after three when we reached Pic River; and having run the boat on to a sandy shore, carried up our things and prepared our camp.

After eight more day's sailing, we reached the Shingwauk again, where a warm welcome awaited us.

CHAPTER XXXVI.

Baptized—Buried.

"I know I shall lie awake at night and grieve at the loss of my boy,—we Indians cannot bear to be parted from our children, but it is right that he should go." Such were the words of the pagan Indian on the shores of Lake Neepigon, when he parted from his loved son Ningwinnena, and gave him up to return with us. I remembered those words,—and often over the camp fire—as we journeyed home I looked across at my adopted son and thought, I will take the very best care I can of you and I trust that by-and-bye it may please God for you to return and do a good work among your people. Such a nice intelligent boy he was,—such gentle eyes, and such a trustful look,—he seemed quite to accept me as his father and guardian, and was always ready to give a helping hand, and he learned with marvellous rapidity. Our arrival at Sault Ste. Marie was quite a new era in his life,— the steamboats, the shops, and people ;—few of course in comparison to places further south—but multitudes compared to the Neepigon region, and he had never seen a horse in his life till he reached the Sault.

It was a great pleasure to me preparing this dear boy for baptism, there were two other pagan lads from Michipicoten and I had them in a class together. I had good reason to hope and believe that all of them embraced the truth and accepted the Lord Jesus as their Saviour. The three boys were baptized by Bishop Fauquier at St. Luke's Church, Sault Ste. Marie, on the 27th of October; the Bishop took a great fancy to Ningwinnena, became his godfather, and gave him his own name, Frederick. Everyone indeed loved the Neepigon boy; he was so gentle in his ways, so quiet and polite in his manner, and made such quaint efforts to converse in English. He seemed so pleased too at any little attention shown him.

But, poor boy, he was soon laid on the bed of sickness. His mother had died of consumption, and that terrible hereditary disease was secretly sapping his life. At Christmas time he was ill with bronchitis and inflammation of the lungs.

From this attack he never thoroughly recovered.

There was a hollowness of the cheek, and an unnatural brightness about the eye, and yet otherwise, he had become well enough again to occupy his place in school and pursue his studies with the other boys. Just after recovering from this illness he wrote a short note in English to the Bishop, composed by himself, in pencil. "Me not learn much book, all the time sick me," and so forth.

Shortly after this he was much delighted at receiving a letter from his father. His poor father spoke of the longing he felt to see his loved son once more, and how anxiously he was looking forward to the spring, when he hoped to see him again. The Bishop also kindly wrote to him in reply to his little letter—exhorting him to try and live as God tells us to do in the Book which He has given to us; and concluding with the earnest hope that when he died, he might go to that happy place where the Saviour Jesus Christ is preparing to receive all who truly love him, "Goodbye, my dear boy," added the Bishop, "may God bless, and make you good." This letter Frederick fondly treasured to the time of his death, and afterwards expressed his desire to see the Bishop again.

On Sunday, March 28th, Frederick was at church in the Sault with the other boys. There was administration of the Holy Communion, and the other boys who had been confirmed remained to partake. Frederick remained with them and innocently came up with the rest to kneel at the rails. I was very sorry to turn him back, but whispered to him in Indian, that only those who were confirmed were about to take the Sacrament, and he quietly withdrew to his seat. Afterwards I explained it to him, and, a day or two subsequently, wrote to the Bishop asking him to arrange, if possible, to hold a confirmation before the boys dispersed for their holidays, so that Frederick, among others, might be confirmed. Had I known that he was so soon to die, and that in his last illness he would not be sufficiently conscious to partake intelligently of the sacred feast, I would not have turned the dear boy back. Too often do we, perhaps, unwittingly act the part of the disciples who hindered the little children in their approach to Jesus.

On Sunday evening, April 27th, Frederick came in for a little talk with me after service. He seemed very earnest and spoke very nicely of his trust in the Saviour. I said to him (in Indian) I want you to get quite well, Frederick, before you go home, perhaps your father will be angry with me if he sees you sick. He looked up in my face to see if I meant what I said, and, seeing me smile, replied, "No, I am sure he will not be angry. He entrusted me to you. My grandfather said, before he died, that we were to wait for an English teacher, and that when he came we must listen to him, and do what he told us. That is why my father gave me up to you."

The dear boy seemed to have some presentiment that he might not live, and expressed himself on the subject in his broken English to one of our little children who had taken him up some canned peaches. "All the time my head just like broke. All the time sick me. By-and-bye I guess me dead."

A few days after, severe symptoms set in, and the doctor was sent for. Frederick became delirious and had to be watched constantly both night and day. We never have any difficulty in procuring night watchers among our Indian boys. Quite a forest of hands generally goes up when the question is put after evening prayers. "Who will stay up to watch to-night?" Two boys stay at a time, and the change is made every three or four hours.

For three days and nights poor Frederick lay in a perfectly unconscious state, taking neither medicine or nourishment. The doctor pronounced it to be organic disease of the brain, the result of a consumptive tendency in his system, and gave but faint hope of his recovery. Day and night we watched him; and were glad when on the fourth day he showed signs of returning consciousness. His brain never seemed to become quite clear, but he had intervals of intelligence, during which he would often answer questions and attempt to repeat verses of Scripture. The verse "Suffer little children to come unto Me," he said through. He attempted also "God so loved the world," but only got as far as "believeth in Him." Two nights before he died, he tried to say the Lord's prayer, but it seemed to be an effort to him; at the words, "as it is in heaven," he stopped, and after a pause, said, " can't say 'my Father.' Too much runaway me."

After a pause I asked him—" Who was it that died on the Cross for us, Frederick?" He rambled for a moment or two, and then, as the meaning of my question flashed upon him, spoke out in clear accents " Jesus Christ." Very little longer was he to live. We had prayed earnestly, constantly, for his recovery, but it was not God's will. On Saturday evening, after prayers, I perceived that he was sinking, and told the boys who were watching him that I did not think he would live through the night. He was breathing heavily and quickly. He would take no notice when spoken to, and could not swallow. An hour or two sped by, it was ten o'clock, and he was now gasping frequently for breath, his pulse being scarcely perceptible. I called to his bedside those boys who had made the Lake Superior trip with me last summer, and we stood watching him. Then as his end drew near, we knelt and I offered up the beautiful commendatory prayer for the sick, and we joined in repeating the Lord's prayer. As we rose from our knees the dear boy gave one more faint gasp for breath and expired. How wonderful are the ways of God, how little can we understand His dealings. But the very essence of faith is the trusting in God when we do not understand His dispensations.

We had earnestly hoped that Frederick's father would have arrived in time to see his boy's body before its burial, and for that reason we kept it twelve days packed in ice, and I wrote to him and sent money for his passage. But it was not so to be. The *Manitoba* arrived at midnight on Wednesday, the 28th of May, but instead of the father, came a letter from him full of expectancy and longing to see his loved son. This seemed to make it sadder still. The letter was dated May 12th; it was written evidently for him by some white man at the Post; and said that he was patiently waiting at Red Rock, with his son Muqua, for Frederick to return; it also enclosed money for the boy's passage on the steamboat.

The day after I received this letter, we buried Frederick. I prepared a slab for his grave, on which were inscribed the words—"*Frederick Oshkahpukeda*, a boy from the wild regions of Lake Neepigon. Was baptized a Christian, Oct. 27th, 1878: and was taken home to his Saviour, May 17th, 1879;—aged fourteen. 'Blessed are the dead which die in the Lord.'" The Bishop read the service at the grave.

Sometime after, I received the following touching

letter from the poor pagan father; written for him by some friend who understood Indian.

"*Red Rock, May 31st,* 1879.

DEAR SIR,—I learn that my poor boy is dead, so that our talk is dead, for I will not send any more of my children to the Home; but if you want to follow out the engagement you made then, put up a schoolhouse somewhere round here, so that our children may learn, for after what has happened I don't think that any of the Indians at Neepigon will let their children go to the Home.

I don't think that we will be able to visit the grave of my poor boy. I would have been very glad if you could have sent the body in the steamer.

I feel very sorry for what has happened, my heart is sore. I do not know what to do.

Did not my poor boy say anything before he died? Surely he said something about his father! If so, let me know when you write. I do not blame anybody about the death of my boy, but I am most happy for the care you have taken with him. I want you to send me an alphabet, and a small book with words of two or three letters, about the school. I have nothing more to say at present. I am very sick at heart. My respects to you, and I hope to see you soon, or hear from you about my son's last words. I would like very much to know.

Your sincere friend,
OSHKAHPUKEDA.

P.S.—Tell all the boys I send them my love; and the boy that he loved best I shall think him my son. Good-bye."

* * * * *

A year after this, Oshkahpukeda, and a number

of the other Indians of Lake Neepigon were baptized; the site for a Mission was selected, and a roughly built log school-house with bark roof was constructed, also another log-house for a teacher. Joseph Esquimau, a pupil of the Shingwauk Home was placed in charge of the Mission temporarily, and conducted services, and taught school very successfully. In the summer of 1881, the Rev. R. Renison, was appointed by the Bishop to take charge of the Mission, and moved there with his family. Several of the Indians had by that time built log-houses for themselves, and the village is called Ningwinnenang, after the boy who died.

CHAPTER XXXVII.

THE WAWANOSH HOME.

THE spot selected for the Wawanosh Home was rather more than a mile above the village of Sault Ste. Marie. I bought five acres of bush land at three pounds an acre as a site for the Institution, and a ten-acre cultivated lot, just opposite, for £60.

Immediately after making the purchase, we took all our boys up there for a "clearing bee;" they hoisted the Union Jack on the site of the new Home, and within a few days had cleared a considerable piece of land and commenced digging the foundations. It was to be a stone building of two storeys high with a frontage of about forty-five feet, and a wing running back, and to cost about £700.

During the summer our boys got out all the stone necessary for building, most of it was collected on the Shingwauk land, and they were paid 20 cents a cord for piling it.

We were anxious as soon as possible to get the new Home into operation. After the summer of 1876 no girls returned to the Shingwauk, and we doubled our number of boys. It seemed hard to shut the girls out from the privileges of Christian care and education, and we were naturally desirous of receiving back as soon as possible those whom we had already commenced teaching. For this reason we thought it well at once to make a beginning by erecting the back wing of the Institution first. During the winter stone and sand were hauled, and on the 5th of May, 1877, building operations commenced. We took the contract ourselves. I had a good practical man as carpenter at the Shingwauk, and we got our plans and specifications; then an estimate was made, and after being approved by a third party—a person experienced in such matters—the work began. Mrs. Fauquier, our Bishop's wife, and two or three other ladies kindly joined with me as a committee to manage the Institution, a lady was engaged as lady Superintendent, a man and wife as gardener and matron, and about the first week in September the girls began to arrive.

We only took ten girls that winter, as we were of course cramped for room.

It was rather uphill work bringing into operation the Wawanosh Home, but difficulties during the progress of a work often have the effect of making it more solid and strong in the end. To induce Sunday Schools and friends to aid us, I divided the estimated cost of the building with its fittings and furniture, into forty-four lots, and a considerable number of these lots were "taken up." Still we were short of money. When the Spring of 1878 came, all our money for building was gone, and the fund to meet current expenses,—even with only ten girls to provide for, was found to be insufficient. It was very discouraging. Sorrowfully I told our lady Superintendent that we must close the Institution for the present,—and sorrowfully I dismissed the girls for their holidays and told them that they must not come back until they heard from me that we were able to receive them.

But God heard our prayers and opened the way for us.

On Sunday Sept. 7th, I had just returned from Garden River where I had been to hold service with the Indians, and on my arrival found a sail-boat lying at our dock. An Indian had come over a hundred miles and had brought five little girls for the Wawanosh Home. Two of them had been with us the winter before and had misunderstood me about coming back, and the other three were new ones,—they all looked so happy and pleased. But their faces fell when I explained to the man our circumstances, that we had closed for want of funds, and could not see our way towards re-opening for the present. The Indian said it seemed very hard to have come such a long distance and then to have to go all the way back again. "Can you not manage to take them," he said; "I will help you all I can,—I will bring you some barrels of fish in the Fall."

I told the man they could all remain with us that night, and I would let him know what could be done after I had thought it over. I went to see Mrs. Fauquier, and the other ladies came together, and we talked it over and had much earnest prayer. It seemed to us all that it was the hand of God pointing out the way, and that we ought to have faith to go on. The end of it was that we kept those five children; the lady who had had charge of the Home the previous winter most generously agreed to remain for another year at a reduced salary and to do without the services of a matron. And so the Wawanosh Home was open again.

Two weeks later I received a letter from England: "I have good news to tell you. Miss —— wrote a few days ago to ask how much money was wanted to complete the Girls' Home. We sent her word that the original estimate was £700, and that about £500 had been collected. I to-day received from her a cheque for £350! Of this £100 is her annual subscription, and £250 for the completion of the Home. You will I am sure look on it as God's gift in answer to the prayer of faith." The following January a letter came from the Indian Department at Ottawa, saying that the Government had in reply to my request, made a grant of £120 towards the building expenses of the Wawanosh Home, and that this grant would be continued annually, provided there were not less than fifteen girls, towards the maintenance of the Institution.

Thus did Almighty God open the way for us, and clear away all our difficulties. By the middle of the summer of 1879 the building was completed, the ground in front cleared and formed into a garden, with a picket fence and two gates, and a drive up to the front door, and at the back a stable, cow-house, pig-styes, &c.

The cottage on the other side of the road was now occupied by Mrs. Bridge, the laundress, and a year or two later we built a new laundry.

The new Home was opened on the 19th of August, 1879, and that winter we had fourteen girls.

The following letter from an English lady who visited the Wawanosh Home in the summer of 1880, gives a good idea of the Institution and its surroundings:—

" I drove to see the Indian girls' Home, and was surprised to find in these wilds such an English stone building, but with the advantage of a nice verandah and green blinds which keep the house cool in summer. The inside of the house I thought very nice; all the rooms are high and of a good size; a hall, school-room, class-room, and dining-room, and prettily furnished sitting-room for the lady superintendent, a laundry, and good kitchen with a large stove—all these are on the ground floor. Upstairs there is a large dormitory with eight double beds and a smaller one with four beds. These rooms are more airy and give more space to each girl than in many institutions I have seen in England. A small room is set apart for the sick. The lavatory is well fitted up, and everything is clean and neat. The girls do the work partly themselves under the matron, and learn to become servants. The Home has only been fully opened a year, so of course it is still rough round the house, but soon the ground will be laid out. On one side of the house will be the vegetable garden, which the girls will be taught to keep weeded and in order. On the other side of the house the committee intend putting up a gymnasium with money a lady in England has collected. It is a room very much wanted, for, in the winter, with the snow three to four, and sometimes five feet deep, it is impossible to send children out, and if they do not get exercise they would suffer. The room is to be 40 feet by 20, with one end divided off for a meat-house and tool-house; when I say a meat-house I mean a place to keep meat, for they kill cattle and sheep enough for the winter at the beginning of the very cold weather, it freezes hard and keeps well. The gymnasium will, when finished, only cost about 200 dollars. The children look very happy and very little amuses them. I showed them some English village children's games, and left them delighted."

There is always a "but," that is, kind friends are wanted to provide for some of the new girls just come to the Home. If any one would give or collect four shillings a week, that is sufficient to feed a child.

CHAPTER XXXVIII.

A Sad Winter.

The winter of 1882 was a sad time. There was great mortality all through the country, and our Homes did not escape.

Our kind friend, Mrs. Fauquier, who, though a constant invalid, had done very much to promote the interests and welfare of our Girls' Home, was called away to the Heavenly Rest on the 4th of November, 1881. During the last few years of her life she had made the Wawanosh Home her special care, her work for Christ. Those girls were always in her thoughts: she it was who devised their uniform dress of blue serge trimmed with scarlet, and got friends in England to supply them; she chose the furniture for the Home and fitted the lady superintendent's rooms so prettily and tastefully. Many were the kind words of counsel that the girls received from her, and it used to be her delight to have them to visit her in the afternoon at the See House.

Only a month had passed after we heard of Mrs. Fauquier's death,—she died in New York,—when the appalling tidings reached us that the Bishop, too, was gone. He had died suddenly in Toronto on December 7th. In the same mail bag which brought the sad news was a letter to me from him, written only an hour or two before he died.

"The sad void," he wrote, "which my dear wife's departure hence has made seems to grow wider and deeper; and it seems difficult to settle down to work as of old. I must try to realize more fully than I have done in the past what a blessing her presence for more than thirty years has been. How true it is that we seldom appreciate our blessings and privileges until they are taken from us."

The church at Sault Ste. Marie was draped with black the following Sunday, and the Indian children of the Homes wore black scarves in token of respect for him who had had their welfare so much at heart.

The next death was that of our carpenter's wife: she had been ailing all through the previous autumn, and died Janaury 2nd.

Then three days later we lost one of the Indian boys, a little fellow named Charlie Penahsewa, who had only been with us a few months. We buried him the next day in our little cemetery at 7 p.m. The boys carried torches.

Several other boys were at this time in the sick room, two or three also of the Wawanosh girls were ill, and the doctor was to and fro at both the Homes.

Poor little Beaconsfield, one of the Michipicotin boys who had been baptized at the same time as Frederick, was among the sick. His only name when he first came to us, nearly five years before, was Chegauns (little man close by); he was a little wild pagan boy, but with soft eyes and gentle disposition, like Frederick, and was very quick to learn. A kind lady in Kingston undertook his support, and took great interest in him, and at her wish we named him "Benjamin Beaconsfield." We had every reason to hope and believe that there was a work of grace in his heart. The little fellow had a tender conscience, and would come and tell me if he had been playing on Sunday or had told an untruth, and would ask me to pray for him. Another boy in the sick room was little Peter, Peterans as we called him [ans at the end of a word makes its diminutive]; he was a grandchild of my old friend, widow Quakegwah, at Sarnia. We sent him and another little fellow who was ailing to the Wawanosh, for change of air and more careful nursing. But it was all in vain. Beaconsfield died on the 16th of January, and little Peter died at the Wawanosh on the 8th of February. They were both buried in our little cemetery.

After this I had to go down to Toronto to attend to diocesan matters, and was away about two months, going through the Muskoka district, and being present in Montreal when the Provincial

Synod met, and our new Bishop, Dr. Sullivan, was unanimously elected.

When I returned to the Shingwauk things looked brighter; the sick room was empty, and every one seemed more cheery. But our hopes were doomed to be disappointed. I had only been home three days when my dear boy, William Sahgucheway, the captain of our school, was taken suddenly ill with inflammation, and a day or two later we were in the greatest alarm about him. I felt about him as I had about Frederick—that surely his life would be spared to us, he of all others was the one whom we looked to as the pride and hope of our Institution; he was nineteen years of age, and was looking forward and preparing for the ministry. But it was not to be. God had called him, and eight days after he was taken ill and died. In the next chapter I shall give a little account of his life.

Three days after William was buried, the bodies of our late dear Bishop and Mrs. Fauquier arrived in charge of two of their sons, it having been their expressed wish to be buried in our little cemetery with our Indian children. On Monday, the 22nd, the long funeral cortège moved slowly to the cemetery. There was a large gathering of people both from the Canadian and American sides— people of all classes and creeds. First, the clergy in their surplices, then the Indian boys, two and two, one of them, who had been supported by the late Bishop, carrying a banner with the words, "He rests from his labours;" then came the hearse bearing the late Bishop's remains, with four horses, all draped, and the Wawanosh girls followed, one of them bearing a banner with the words, "She is not dead, but sleepeth;" then the hearse, and members of the family and other mourners—a long mournful procession. A vault had been prepared, and the coffins, covered with flowers, were laid within it, and the latter part of the Burial Service read. Thus the good, kind-hearted, self-sacrificing Bishop, the first Bishop of this wild Missionary diocese, and his afflicted yet devoted wife, who had laboured so earnestly for the welfare of the Indians during the latter part of their lives, were now laid side by side in the Indian cemetery to await the joyful resurrection to eternal life.

The very next grave to the Bishop's was that of Frederick, the Neepigon boy.

Before the summer holidays commenced, the cemetery gate had once more to be opened and the earth once more to be turned, for another boy, Simon Altman, from Walpole Island, was dead. This was the fifth boy who had died during the winter, not from any malignant disease or fever, but from various causes, and seven bodies in all had been committed to the silent dust. For a time we were afraid that the saddening effect of so many deaths would lead to a complete break up of our work, as the Indians are of course very superstitious and might be afraid to send any more of their children to us.

Next autumn our number at both the Homes was very much reduced, still we were able to keep on, and now our pupils are once more steadily on the increase.

CHAPTER XXXIX.

WILLIAM SAHGUCHEWAY.

WILLIAM SAHGUCHEWAY was born on the Indian Reserve of Walpole Island about the year 1862, the exact date is not known. His father and mother both died eight or ten years ago, and since then he had lived with an uncle and aunt, of both of whom he was very fond. He had two younger brothers, but no sisters. One of the brothers, Elijah, was a pupil with William at the Shingwauk Home for two or three years. He left when the Home was temporarily closed in the spring of 1880, and before it had re-opened he had been called home to his Saviour. William felt the death of his little brother very deeply. In a letter dated June 4th he says, "Last Sunday my brother Elijah died: but now he is with Jesus and the angels. This text he had in his Bible, 'Blessed are the dead which die in the Lord' (Rev. xiv. 13); and also the Bible was dated May 30th, 1879.. This is important to me, like if it were telling me how he died and when he died."

William Sahgucheway came first to the Shingwauk Home on the 17th of June, 1875. I had paid a visit to Walpole Island that summer, and William was one who, in company with five or six other children, came back with me to Sault Ste. Marie. He was at that time a bright, intelligent looking lad of twelve or thirteen years of age, and being an orphan, he was made rather a special favourite from the first; the attachment grew, and soon the boy learned to look upon me as his father, and always commenced his letters "My dear Noosa" (father) when writing to me. William like the other boys in the Institution, was supported by the contributions of Sunday-school children, and it was quite hoped that he would at no distant day have become a student at Huron Theological College.

William's Indian name was "Wahsashkung"—shining light. A most appropriate name, for his presence always seemed to bring light and happiness; he was always so cheerful, so ready to help, so self-denying; grown people and little children were equally his friends. We always regarded that verse in Matt. v. as specially his verse,—"Let your light so shine before men, that they may see your good works and glorify your Father which is in heaven."

William accompanied me on many of my travels. He was with me on the shores of Lake Neepigon in 1878, when that pagan tribe was discovered, who for thirty years had been waiting for a Missionary to come to them. He befriended the pagan boy, Ningwinnena, and taught him to pray and love his Saviour. And when the poor boy died at Christian, six months after entering the Institution, William was among those who knelt at his bedside and watched his last expiring breath. In 1879 William accompanied me to England, and while there wrote a little journal of his travels, extracts from which were published. Wherever he went he made friends, and many white people on both sides of the Atlantic will long remember his bright, intelligent face, his gentle voice, and kind obliging manner.

In the spring of 1880, when I was dangerously ill and my life despaired of, William was one of the few Indian boys who were privileged to come to my bedside, and the only one who was allowed to take turn in watching beside me at night; for whenever there was anything to be done requiring special effort or care, it was always William who was wanted, and William who was ready.

About three years before this time the dear boy became truly in earnest about religion, and dedicated his life to the Saviour. From his earliest boyhood he would appear to have been a child of grace, avoiding what was bad, with a desire to follow what was pure and good; but with nearly all followers of Christ there is probably some period in life which may be looked back to when the seeds of truth began more distinctly to germinate in the soul, and that blessed union with the Saviour, which is the joy of all true believers, was for the first time perhaps fully realized and felt. It was on the 23rd March, 1877, that this dear boy, William, after a long earnest talk, knelt down beside me and yielded his heart to the Saviour: "Tabaningayun Jesus, kemeenin ninda noongoom suh tebekuk, kuhnuhga kayahhe che tebanindezosewaun keen dush chetebanemeyun"—"Lord Jesus, I give my heart to Thee this night, no longer to belong to myself, but to belong to Thee." I gave him a Bible the same evening, and it became his most valued treasure; on the first leaf is the verse, "Him that cometh unto Me, I will in no wise cast out," and on the last leaf, "God is love."

I always tried to impress on those who had dedicated themselves to the Saviour's service, that they should prove the fact of their union with

Christ by working for Him and bearing fruit to the glory of His name. William seemed to be especially impressed with this, and rarely a week passed without his trying to exercise some influence for good among his companions. Many are the boys now in the Institution who can trace their first serious thoughts on their spiritual condition to his intercourse with them. In January, 1878, a boys' prayer meeting was commenced weekly, and continued almost without interruption, except during holidays. The boys met on Wednesday evenings after prayers—quite by themselves—one read a portion of Scripture in his own language, and others offered a few words of simple prayer. It was due to William and one or two like-minded companions that these little gatherings were kept together, and there can be little doubt that much blessing resulted.

William used latterly to take notes of the sermons which he heard on Sundays.

And now we come to the last scenes of the dear boy's life here on earth.

I had been away on a tour through the other dioceses, and William, as captain of the school, had additional duties devolving upon him during the principal's absence. He had charge of the clothing store and had to give out clothing each week to the boys, and perform other duties requiring care and attention. The bodies of the late Bishop Fauquier and Mrs. Fauquier were expected shortly to arrive for interment in the Shingwauk cemetery, and preparations had to be made for this; the road to the cemetery, which was blocked in places by large boulders and old pine stumps, had to be cleared and levelled. William, of course, was called into service for this—no one could clear a road through a rough tract of land better than he. He was busy preparing for the spring examinations, and very anxious to be victor; but books were laid aside without a murmur, and he shouldered his pickaxe and shovel, and in company with two or three other big boys set cheerfully and heartily to work. It seemed strange that his last work on earth should be preparing this road to the cemetery along which his own body would be carried before those of the Bishop and Mrs. Fauquier arrived. That hard work, with taking a chill, was probably in some measure the cause of his death. He seemed very well on the Friday, the day on which I returned home, and joined the boys in offering a hearty welcome, but the following Sunday he seemed to be ailing, and on Monday, although he had come down to lessons, and was setting to work, he was trembling and scarcely able to stand. I recommended him to return to his room to bed, which he at once did, but it was very soon evident that a serious illness was setting in. An Indian woman was engaged to nurse him, and the doctor from the Sault attended him. For the first few days no great alarm was felt, and the pain seemed to be in some measure subdued. No one would allow himself to imagine that death was so near. It was not until Friday evening, the 12th, that a decided change for the worse set in. He became very low and weak, with a slight tendency to delirium. We were all very anxious, and the Indian boys took turns watching at his bedside. On Sunday afternoon ten or twelve of the boys came up to his room for prayer. William, though very weak, and only able to say a few words at a time, asked permission to speak to them, and he spoke very earnestly for six or seven minutes in his own language; then we knelt and prayed—prayed with great earnestness that God, if it were His holy will, would permit our dear boy to recover. All Monday he was very ill. Our hopes were sinking. It scarcely seemed possible that the dear boy could live more than another day or two. We had much earnest prayer at his bedside, and the faintest signs of improvement were eagerly looked for. He was quite resigned to God's will, wishing to recover if it were his Father's will, or ready to die if the call had come. In the afternoon he seemed to realize that his end was drawing near. To one who visited him and remained a short time alone with him he said, "I should like to meet my little brother Elijah again; I do so love Elijah." And after a pause he said, "I don't think I shall live long, I am getting very weak." "We all love you very much," was replied, "we indeed wish to keep you with us, but God's will must be done." "Yes," he said, "God's will must be done. May be God will revive me, but I have no wish whether to live or die. I wish for what is God's will." "Is there anything you want?" was asked. "No—thank you," he replied with great effort, then put his hand to his heart and slowly waved it upwards. "I shall soon be singing on the golden shore," he said. To one of our little girls who came in he said, "Do you like to see me like this, Winnie?" "No," said the little child, the tears trickling down her cheeks. "Perhaps I will get well again if it is God's will," he said, "but I don't know." To the carpenter, who had lost his wife only a few months before, he spoke very earnestly: "You see," he said, "there is nothing to trouble me, nothing at all; God is love, this is all God's love to me; may be God will take me away." "Poor boy, poor boy," ejaculated the carpenter, with tears in his eyes, "how you are changed; how much you must have suffered." "Oh, it is just nothing," said William; "God is love, I can trust in Him: 'the blood—of Jesus Christ—cleanseth us—from all sin.'"

I could hardly bear to speak to him of death,— it seemed to me as though he must live, that a change for the better would set in, and that the dear boy would revive. I repeated some passages of Scripture to him and knelt often for prayer. Many, indeed, were the earnest prayers that went up to the throne of grace for the boy's recovery.

Between eleven and half-past he was left for the night in charge of two Indian boys, Kahgaug and Willis. They were to keep hot bricks to his hands and feet, and administer a stimulating mixture and nourishment, and at two o'clock their place would be taken by two other boys. Having been up a great part of the preceding night, I then retired to rest, to be called if there was any change for the worse.

Just at half-past two there came a knock at the door,—"William is worse; please come at once."

I hurried up to the sick room as quickly as possible, but it was a moment too late—the dear boy had breathed his last. His hands were clasped on his breast, his eyes lifted to heaven, a smile just fading on his lips, and thus he had left the earth and gone to meet his Saviour. Three boys only were with him when he died—Wigwaus, Benjamin, and Davidans. We knelt together, and I offered up prayer, humbly commending the soul of the dear brother departed into the hands of Almighty God, as into the hands of a faithful Creator and most merciful Saviour.

A feeling of awe seemed to pervade the whole household when, at early dawn, the tolling of the school-bell told only too plainly that the beloved spirit had departed. Never was a boy more loved by his play-mates or more honoured and respected by his teachers. As he lived he died, trusting in the merits of an Almighty Saviour for his salvation.

On the evening of his death his dear form was laid by loving hands in the coffin, and some white flowers placed on his breast; the lid was drawn back a little, and on it were placed his Prayer-book, his Bible (open at 1 John iv.), a photograph of him in a frame, and a single wax taper. Then the folding doors leading into the back school-room were opened and the boys gathered around and sang the hymn he loved, " Safe in the arms of Jesus." Scarcely an eye was dry, and many a sigh was heaved, and many a sob broke the silence of the apartment as they came up one by one to look on the marble face of their dead companion, and to imprint a kiss on his cold brow. Many of the boys would not be satisfied with coming once; they came again and again, and some laid their faces down on his and sobbed. Several hymns were sung: " Here we suffer grief and pain," " There is a happy land," and " My God, my Father, while I stray," and prayer also was offered.

The funeral was on Thursday, Ascension day, at nine o'clock in the morning. The coffin was brought into the school-room by six boys, who had been appointed pall-bearers, and I read the opening sentences of the burial service and special psalms and lessons; then, after a hymn, was the sermon, from 1 John iii. 2, " We know that when He shall appear, we shall be like Him, for we shall see Him as He is," and I read some extracts from William's diary, which he had commenced keeping four years before; they show what the boy's thoughts were and how near he lived to his Saviour.

Jan. 27, 1878.—" O Lord Jesus Christ, I have given my heart to Thee. I belong to Thee, and I want to work for Thee as long as I live. Give me Thy Holy Spirit in mine heart. May I not get cold and careless, but may I always be full of love to Thee. May I not be a dead branch, but may I bear much fruit to the glory of Thy name. Amen."

March 5.—" O Lord Jesus Christ, give me Thy Holy Spirit that I may be able to fight the temptations of the world, the flesh, and the devil."

Oct. 1.—" O God, I give my body unto Thee, and wherever you want me to go, I will go, and whatever you want me to do as long as I live, I shall do this for the name of Christ."

March 21, 1879.—" O Lord, I am trying to work for Thee. Am I trying to walk in the light every day? Am I going to serve God or serve the devil? Let me not think too much of the things of this world. Let me more think about the things of heaven. This is all,—for Christ's sake."

After another hymn had been sung, a procession was formed to the cemetery, and the dear boy's body was laid in the grave, earth to earth, ashes to ashes, dust to dust, in sure and certain hope of a glorious resurrection to eternal life.

There was one more duty to be performed on the return of the funeral party to the school-room, and that was to distribute some of the dear boy's books and treasures to those who would specially value them. I took for my share the Bible which I had given him four years before, and an ancient arrow head, which he had dug up while making the road to the cemetery, and had laughingly remarked that he would keep it till he died. The rest of the things were packed in a box and sent home to his aunt.

Who shall estimate the amount of good done by this earnest whole-souled Indian boy during his short career? He sowed good seed, and we trust there may be an abundant harvest in the hearts and lives of the other boys. When asked how many of them had received special benefit by their intercourse with William, twenty boys rose to their feet. Many testified that they had been spoken to by him of the Saviour, others that they had been checked by him in doing something sinful, others, that he had talked or read or offered prayer with them. What a blessed testimony, that in a school of fifty-four boys, twenty should have been benefited by the example and teaching of one boy who loved the Saviour! May God the Holy Spirit bless this simple recital to the hearts of those who read it, and may other boys, whether white or Indian, be stirred in their souls to follow the example of this young soldier of the cross, and let their light shine before men as did this young Indian boy—Wahsashkung—Shining light—William Sahgucheway.

CHAPTER XL.

Our Indian Homes.

Come and visit our Indian Homes now, this summer of 1884. No longer are we in the midst of bush and swamp, as we were ten years ago. The land has been cleared up and a good part of it brought under cultivation, fences have been put up, and several new buildings added. Let us visit the Shingwauk Home first. We may go by water, and land at the Shingwauk dock; there is the boat-house, with our new boat, *The Missionary*, given to us by the children of St. James's Sunday-school, Toronto, floating gently on the dark water within. We have no need to walk up to the Institution. There is an excellent tramway, which has just been completed, and visitors are requested to take their seats in the tramcar, and some of the Indian boys will push them up to the Home. We can already see the Institution over the brow of the hill, and a little to the right the Memorial Chapel, and nearer to us the Factory, and off to the left the boot shop and carpenter's cottage. We note that there are neat stone walls round some of the fields, and a white picket fence inclosing the Institution; the old-fashioned lych-gate in front of the Chapel also strikes us, with the hops clambering over it; but we must hasten on and enter the Home. As we walk up the central drive we notice that the Institution is a substantial stone building, the bareness of the walls relieved by a pretty trellis-work, up which hops and other creeping plants are climbing; to our right is a cottage-wing, which is the principal's residence, and to our left the entrance hall, with an ornamental belfry over it; a little further to our left is another small stone building —the dairy. We enter the hall, and, having written our names in the Visitors' book, we ascend the oak staircase and visit the school-room. Here the boys are all busy at work with their slates and books, and Mr. Wotton, the master, is instructing a class by the black-board. The school-room is nicely fitted up with modern desks and other appliances; on the walls are large maps and pictures, which give it a cheerful look; the ceiling is panelled in woods of two shades. Opening into the school-room is a smaller room, a class-room separated from it by three folding-doors. Ascending the staircase, we visit the dormitories. The east dormitory for the senior boys is fitted with English iron bedsteads, the junior dormitory has wooden bedsteads painted blue, and wide enough for two little fellows to sleep in each; the front dormitory, which is the largest of them all, is hung with hammocks,— there is sleeping accommodation altogether for about sixty-five boys. Descending once more, we pass through the lavatory and the matron's sitting-room down to the dining-hall, and we note as we go along every here and there a shelf with three white pails full of water and an ominous F painted on them. Evidently experience has taught caution. The dining-hall is a fine large room, the ceiling panelled like the school-room. It has five long tables, at each of which twelve or fourteen boys can sit comfortably. One side of the room we notice is railed off—this is called the pen, and here the boys have to wait in patience while the tables are prepared for meals. Adjoining the dining-hall are the kitchen on one side, the work-room on the other. Every thing looks clean and tidy and well kept—the matron takes pride in having her department all in good order. In the work-room we find the Indian servant, Eliza, working at the sewing-machine making garments for the boys. Passing on through the other doorway, we cross a passage, and enter the class-room where John Esquimau is sitting at his studies, reading theology and studying Latin and Greek, with a view to entering the ministry. Adjoining this room is the office and dispensary.

And now we must leave the Institution building and visit the Chapel (see Frontispiece), a little winding path under the trees leads us to it. The building is of stone, set in a frame-work of wood, which, painted dark, gives a most picturesque appearance. There is a deep porch at the western entrance with stained glass window; within are heavy oak doors with ornamental mountings, and these, being opened, give us a view of the interior of the Chapel, and a very pretty view it is. In front of us are pillars supporting the chancel arch, and on either side a smaller arch, one enclosing the vestry, the other the organ-chamber; the space between the top of these arches and the roof being filled with fretwork. The windows are stained glass. The pulpit and prayer-desk and all the seats are of oak, and nicely carved. Under the chancel window is an oak reredos, on which are inscribed the Creed, the Lord's Prayer, and the Ten Commandments in Indian. The altar-cloth is a very handsome one, given by a lady in England, and the stone font was presented by relatives of the late Bishop. Service is held in the Chapel twice every Sunday, the pupils from both Homes attending; and on Wednesday evenings there is a short service and catechizing.

R

Crossing to the other side of the road after leaving the Chapel, we enter the sash and door factory, and are immediately deafened by the din of the various machines in motion. Three Indian boys are at work here under the foreman, making doors, window-sash mouldings, and turned work of all descriptions. The boys are old pupils who have passed through the Institution, and now receive wages for their work, but they attend school every evening, which is a great advantage to them. One or two of the younger boys are also commencing to learn carpenter work at the factory. Crossing to the other cottage to the left of the Institution, we enter the boot shop; here we find another old pupil at work,—Harry Nahwa-quageezhik,—and a very good boot maker he is. He does all the work for the Institutions, both mending and making, and has one or two younger boys under his instruction. When not required at the boot shop, Harry goes to garden or farm work.

And now we must drive out to the Wawanosh Home and pay it a visit also. It is upwards of two miles from Shingwauk, up the northern road and away from the river. As we drive up the road bordered with fields of grain or grass on either side, or shaded by birch and fir trees, we catch sight of the stone building to our right, in a nest of green foliage; and on the left white garments flapping in the breeze bespeak the presence of the laundry, with the laundress' cottage close beside. A number of the girls are on the verandah, or amusing themselves on the grass, for it is play-time and school is over. Miss Cunningham the lady Superintendent, meets us at the door, and conducts us through the building; on the left as we enter are the school-room and work-room with folding doors between, and on the right Miss Cunningham's little sitting-room, and the girls' dining-room; then at the back are the kitchen and wash-house, and overhead the girls' dormitories and lavatory and other bed-rooms. All is kept very clean and neat, and does credit to those who are in charge.

Such are our buildings and our work, and such the efforts that we are making for the evangelization and training of these poor Ojebway Indians.

And now perhaps the question will be asked:—

DO THESE INDIAN HOMES SEEM LIKELY TO PROVE A SUCCESS?

Have we reason to expect that we shall, in due time, achieve our object, and raise the Indian to a position equal to that of his white brethren? Is this idea of inducing them to exchange the bow and arrow for the carpenter's bench, the war-club for the blacksmith's hammer, the net and canoe for the plough, a mere visionary one, or is it a scheme that we have a good prospect of seeing carried into effect? The following questions suggest themselves and we are prepared with the answers:—

1. Are the Indians willing to make the change? Yes, for the most part, they desire it.

2. Are their sons capable of receiving education and acquiring a knowledge of the various trades sufficient to make a livelihood? We refer to the appended letters from the masters of the various trades that our boys are learning: and as to education, our own experience is that Indian boys can learn as fast as white boys, and many of them will *retain* what they have learnt a good deal better. They read distinctly, without any foreign accent,

write a capital hand, and are very fair arithmeticians.

3. Will they stick to their work? Yes. We were doubtful about this at first, but now we can say yes. Our apprentice boys work ten hours a day, six days a week, and very rarely ask for a holiday. Having once become accustomed to regular work, they like it, and will stick to it as well as any white man.

4. Will their love for a wild life ever be eradicated? Perhaps not. Why should it? Our boys, all of them, thoroughly enjoy a "camp out," such as we have sometimes in the summer, but scarcely one of them would wish to go back and spend his whole life in this manner. They know that a life depending on hunting and fishing means poverty, dirt, and ignorance; and they don't mean to go back to this. We don't wish to un-Indianize them altogether, we would not overcurb their free spirit; we would not pluck the feather from their cap or the sash from their waist or the moccasin from their foot. They are a proud, grand nation in their way. An Indian was never a slave any more than a Briton. An Indian has no words of profanity in his language. An Indian is noted for his loyalty to the British Crown. Let them hand down their noble and good qualities to their children. But in the matter of procuring a livelihood let us, for their own good, induce them to lay aside the bow and fish-spear, and, in lieu thereof, put their hand to the plough, or make them wield the tool of the mechanic.

We hope to see the day, if it please God, when these Indian Homes shall be three times their present size, and the number of the pupils deriving benefit from them shall be three-fold increased.

The tailor to whom one boy was apprenticed writes as follows:—

"DEAR SIR,—Aubee has all the necessary qualifications to make a good tailor. I think it would be better for him to come every week, instead of every second week, as at present.
Yours &c.,
W. VAUGHAN."

From the Printer.

"The Indian boys who are employed in the Shingwauk Printing Office—in charge of which I have been for the past eighteen months—have, during that time, made very considerable progress. I have found them, as a rule, apt, obedient, steady and clever, and do not doubt, that in course of time and with proper education, they will make excellent printers.
S. REID."

From the Tinsmith.

"DEAR SIR,—I think that you have not a boy in the Home better deserving of praise than Pedahjewun. He will make a first-class tinsmith. He has been with me two years and I never knew him to tell me a lie in that time.
H. P. PIM."

From the Carpenter and Builder.

"SIR,—From the time Jackson has been under me, he has learnt the trade fast. He is fond of it, is steady and obliging, and I think will make a good mechanic as joiner and carpenter.
Yours truly,
E. MURTON (Builder)."

CHAPTER XLI.

A Pow-wow at Garden River.

The following is an account of a visit paid by the Bishop and Mrs. Sullivan to Garden River, where Indian names were conferred on them:—

Garden River was reached about 6 p.m. on Saturday, August 29th, the tent pitched, the vacant Mission house occupied, fires lighted, water brought from the river, and other preparations made for the night, the boys of the party voting, with true tramp-like instinct, that they preferred slumbering in the new mown hay in the barn. After tea under the shade of a spreading pine tree, the Bishop and myself spent some time visiting the Indian houses, among them that of an old man of eighty, who had been blind for four years, but bore his affliction, augmented as it was by other trials, with an uncomplaining submission. Another dwelling visited was that of Chief Buhkwujjenene, already known to our readers. On the table his Indian Testament lay open, his constant study, in which, he told the Bishop, he had taught himself to read his own tongue.

At 9 p.m. all assembled in the little church, and there, by the light of "a lantern dimly burning," and amid a holy calm, unbroken save by the rustling of the leaves at the open windows, joined in the evening sacrifice of prayer and praise.

Soon after breakfast next morning the tinkling of the church bell was heard, and groups of two or three were seen assembling, and passing into the sacred building, with a quiet, silent reverence. The service, with the exception of the Old Testament lesson and the sermon, which was interpreted, was in Ojebway, and old and young listened attentively as the preacher told the story of the Brazen Serpent, and pointed his hearers to Him who said of Himself, " I, if I be lifted up, will draw all men unto Me."

At 3 p.m. the bell was rung, the flags hoisted, and the whole party ushered into the school-house to find the platform furnished with chairs, the centre one carefully reserved for the " Kechemakadawekoonuhya " (the big black coat). By the time the feast was over the sun was setting. Now the table was put aside, benches arranged, and the signal for the pow-wow, given on the drum, when all who could find space to sit or stand crowded in. A few minutes' silence followed, and then Chief Buhkwujjenene rose, advanced to the platform, shook hands (an invariable preliminary to an Indian speech), and said, " Chiefs, principal men, brothers, and sisters, we were told many days ago that our new Bishop was coming among us, and we decided to have a cup of tea with him. Now he has come, and has eaten and drank with us. Now (turning to the Bishop) we are glad that you have come, and that you have told us the Gospel." His way being paved by this brief introduction, the Bishop addressed them, saying that he thanked them for the feast they had prepared, and the very kind welcome they had given to him. When Jesus Christ was on earth, Matthew the publican and others made feasts for Him, and as the Indians had received him in Christ's name and for His sake, therefore they would receive the fulfilment of the promise which Christ gave, that " whosoever gave to a disciple a cup of cold water only should in no wise lose his reward." At his last visit he told them he would go to school and learn their language; and he had done this, and as he had a good teacher, Mr. Wilson, he had been able to read part of their beautiful services yesterday in their own tongue : it was a hard language to learn, but he would persevere until he was able to preach to them. He had some good news to tell them about their church. A gentleman in Toronto, whom he had never seen, had sent him 50 dollars in aid of it (great clapping of hands), and more, he was sure, was on the way, for God never failed to hear and help His children who prayed to Him in their trouble and difficulty. He had heard that they were going to give him a new name. He had had two names already, first Edward Sullivan, then Edward Algoma, and he hoped that the new one would be a good one, and that he would not be ashamed to tell it his friends and theirs in Montreal and Toronto.

After this the other old Chief, a fine looking specimen of the aboriginal race, rose from his seat, and, divesting himself of his loose scarlet jacket, put on a fantastic head-dress composed of eagle feathers, then threw round his neck a blue ribbon with a heavy silver medal suspended from either end (one presented to his father by George III., and the other to himself by the Prince of Wales). Then fastening on his right wrist an armlet made of polecat skins, he stepped on to the platform, and apologizing for the lack of a portion of his costume, on account of the excessive heat, proceeded in highly poetic strains, and with a fervid, impassioned manner, to which no description could do justice, to picture the glory of the rising sun, how at first the night is dark, very dark, and the darkness clears a little, and the light looks through, and the great sun appears, creeping up slowly higher and higher, from east to west, till the whole heaven is filled with his brightness, making all things glad—" so," said the old Chief, turning suddenly to the Bishop, " has your teaching been, and our hearts are glad because of the new light, and henceforth you will be called 'Tabahsega,' *i.e.*, ' spreading or radiant light.' " Here he extended his hand, and said, " Boozhoo (*i.e.*, good day) Tabahsega," a salutation which was re-echoed by the others, who, coming forward in succession, repeated the ceremony of hand-shaking. The old Chief then beckoned to the Bishop's wife to come forward, and going back to his former figure, to bring out the idea of the soft roseate hue that overspreads the sky before the rising of the sun, announced that her name should be " Misquahbenooqua " (*i.e.*, rosy dawn), at which there was great applause, and a number of squaws came forward and confirmed the title given by going through the hand-shaking process again. The evening was by this time far advanced, but there still remained a part of the ceremony which could not possibly be dispensed with. This was the smoking of the pipe of peace. The pipe was no ordinary one, but about four feet long, the bowl carved of stone, and the stem of wood in spiral form, dyed with alternate lines of red and blue. With this in his hand, duly prepared and lit, old Shingwauk stood in the centre of the group, and, first taking a few preliminary whiffs (for the pipe to go out before all have smoked is unlucky), presented it to each of the guests, beginning with the Bishop, who performed his part as well as could be expected of one who was a stranger to the art, the others following his example, so far, at least in some cases, as putting the pipe to their lips. This being the last scene in this interesting drama, the Bishop addressed a few parting words of counsel to those present, through the interpreter, expressing the hope that, as they had feasted together very happily on earth, they might be permitted, in God's mercy, to sit down together at the marriage supper of the Lamb. He then concluded with a collect and the benediction in Indian, after which our kind and hospitable entertainers dispersed to their homes, and the visitors returned by boat to Sault Ste. Marie.

CHAPTER XLII.

Glad Tidings from Neepigon.

I shall now close this little volume with a letter from the Rev. R. Renison, who is labouring most devotedly among the poor Neepigon Indians. It is dated February, 1884, and it speaks for itself.

"On Monday, Feb. 12th, Oshkahpukeda and myself left Ningwinnenang to visit a family of pagan Indians about forty miles from this Mission. Our blankets, overcoats, provisions, and cooking utensils, made a pack of forty pound weight for each to carry; over lakes, through the dense bush, up steep hills which were sometimes almost insurmountable. It was one of the most beautiful winter mornings that I have ever yet experienced. The sun shone brightly, and it was just cold enough to render a brisk walk enjoyable. At 11 a.m. we reached a wigwam at the north end of McIntyre Bay, which was occupied by Mishael Obeseekun, their wives and children, who had left the Mission some time previous for the purpose of snaring rabbits, which at present is the chief support of the Indians. Here we received a hearty welcome; a large pot of rabbits was quickly cooked—we enjoyed them thoroughly; and all the little children declared that they were glad to see their Missionary. Mishael's wife having noticed that my moccasin was badly torn, took her needle and thread and had it fixed 'in less than no time.'

Before leaving I took the Indian New Testament and read the following verse:—'This is a faithful saying and worthy of all acceptation that Christ Jesus came into the world to save sinners, of whom I am chief.' I find it a good plan, when reading to the Indians, to take one text at a time. They differ very much from the white people in this respect, as you may read it over and over twenty times and yet they will be glad to hear it again. The result of this plan is, that many of the Indians at our Mission have committed to memory several verses. I was much astonished as well as delighted a few days ago to find that Obeseekun could repeat accurately ten texts.

Well, at 2 p.m. we reached 'Kookookuhooseebee' (owl river). We followed this river for about half an hour, and then entered the bush. We walked till sun down, and then camped near the shore of Black Sturgeon Lake. We had a splendid fire, as there was plenty of dry pine close at hand. We ate heartily, but slept little, as the night was very cold. We had breakfast by moonlight, and then recommenced our journey.

Our route lay through the middle of the lake, which is about ten miles long. As we again entered the bush at its north end, to our great astonishment we met the very pagan Indian whom we were so anxious to see. He had a small tebaugan drawn by one dog—was on his way to the 'Neepigon Post' for pork and flour. His wife and children were very hungry, rabbits and fish this winter being so scarce that several of the Indians are obliged to abandon their usual hunting grounds.

'Kebuk,' for this is the pagan's name, was very glad to see us, a large fire was quickly made, snow melted, pork fried, and soon the Missionary, guide, and pagan were enjoying a hearty meal.

About two years ago, and upon two different occasions, I had visited this pagan family. I tried to preach Christ to them the Saviour of all men. I must confess that after twice travelling a distance of eighty miles through the dense bush, that I was a little discouraged and depressed in spirits to find that the invitation was refused, and full and free salvation through the precious blood of Jesus rejected.

And now for the third time the Missionary and pagan meet face to face. He knows full well the errand on which I have come. As we sat for a few minutes in silence around the blazing fire I prayed to my Father in secret to enlighten his understanding, and give him grace to receive the Gospel message and enter the fold of the Good Shepherd.

'Owh suh kadabwayandung kuhya kabaptizooind tahbemahjeah, owh duhyabwendusig tahnahneboomah.' ('He that believeth and is baptized shall be saved, and he that believeth not shall be condemned.') The once proud pagan now kneels in prayer; he receives Christ rejoicingly; accepts this time, the Gospel invitation. 'Proceed on your journey,' said he, 'go to my wigwam, baptize all my children, and next spring, when navigation opens, I will go to the Mission and myself and wife will be baptized in the church at Ningwinnenang. This is my wish, I will build a house on the Mission ground, and am very anxious that my children should be properly instructed.' After bidding us a friendly 'boozhoo,' he proceeded on his journey to the Neepigon Post, and we hastened toward the wigwam from which we were still ten miles distant.

At about 3 p.m. we reached Muskrat Lake, which is four miles long. On the opposite shore we saw the pagan's daughter fishing for pike with hook and line under the ice. When she first noticed us approaching, she quickly disappeared in the bush, entered the wigwam and apprized them of our coming.

When we arrived we found eight pagans, including two old women of 80 and 75 years old, one girl and four children. After many friendly 'boozhoos' and hearty expressions of welcome, the Missionary and guide seated on shingoob branches rested their wearied limbs beside a blazing fire, whilst the two old women smoking their pipes and preparing rabbits and pike for dinner, were heard to say 'pooch tah pukedawaug pooch tah-kadishkhusk-enawug' (they must be very hungry and must have a hearty meal). After dinner the Indian New Testament was introduced, the simple Gospel expounded and some of Christ's beautiful invitations read. I tried to prove to them from God's own Word that we all need a Saviour, for that all have sinned and come short of the glory of God; that there is one way only by which we can be saved, namely, by entering the fold of the good Shepherd; that Jesus Christ himself is the door, 'He that believeth and is baptized shall be saved.'

It appears that nearly two months ago these nine pagans had unanimously agreed to become Christians and join our mission at Ningwinnenang. The seed sown two years ago was not sown in vain, the bread cast upon the waters is found after many days, God's word will not return to Him void. One of the old women, 80 years old, with only one eye, determines to return with the Missionary, a distance of 40 miles through the dense bush and over frozen lakes, to be instructed at the Mission and prepared for baptism. The young woman and four children were baptized. The rest of the family, namely an old man of 75, 'Kebuk,' and his wife will (D.V.) be baptized in the spring in our little church, and then we hope to have quite a nice congregation.

In conclusion, let me add that poor old Wesqua, who returned with us to the Mission, has not yet recovered from the fatigue of the journey, the last day's travelling in particular for her was very trying. We had to cross an arm of the lake about 15 miles in breadth, and the piercing north wind was too much for an old woman of 80, whose entire clothing consisted of an old canvass bag rent in two and rolled around her legs for leggings, her skirts of blue calico did not reach much below her knees, and a piece of old blanket thrown over her head and shoulders was all that she had to save her from the sharp wind which blows at intervals across the Neepigon Lake. When she arrived the blood had almost ceased to circulate, her hands were numb, and she was indeed in a pitiable condition. Half a teaspoonful of stimulant in a cup of warm water was all we had to give. She revived, and after a supper of bread and tea was soon herself again.

Let me ask some of my Christian friends to whom 'the lines have fallen in pleasant places' to remember the poor Indians at Neepigon. Cast off warm clothing even of an inferior quality, will be thankfully received and gratefully acknowledged; and we trust that those who cannot assist us from a pecuniary point of view will at least remember us in their prayers."

THE END.

Printed at the University Press, Oxford
By HORACE HART, *Printer to the University*

www.ingramcontent.com/pod-product-compliance
Lightning Source LLC
Chambersburg PA
CBHW021407230426
43666CB00006B/667